The History of Taekwondo; an outsider's perspective

By

Matt Scott Diaz

©Matt Scott Diaz 2014

New Preface, Introduction, Afterthoughts, and Conclusion ©2018

Text by author. All images/photos by author or are public domain.

A very special thanks to all of the instructors, training partners, students, and competitors in the martial arts *who are still a part of my life* – God bless!

Contents:

Preface…………………………………………………………………...…..4

Introduction…………………………………………..………………………...5

The History of Taekwondo………………………………………………….10

Afterthoughts………………………………………………………………...48

Conclusion……………………………………………………………………57

Annotated Bibliography ……………………………………………………59

Preface

It started out as nothing more than just an assignment. Within a short period of training in Taekwondo I had qualified to take the coveted black belt test with one of the requirements being writing an essay. It was a mere formality as no one was going to truly examine the work and dissect the information. Most candidates simply picked from one of five questions and scribble out a quick three page essay. While most people felt the essay portion was the most dreaded portions of the test, I approached it as I approach most things in life… as a challenge!

I've often lived my life as the words of the famous Frank Sinatra song stated; *All or nothing at all.* If I was going to pass a black belt test I was going to put the same amount of effort that I put into my physical training into the essay. The result turned what was supposed to be a simple essay into a research thesis on the history of Taekwondo. I felt that the history of the art needed to be told from a true historic perspective. There were a myriad of books on Taekwondo with usually a short section on the origins. But the sections were all too brief and generally focused on what could be deemed as the "general consensus" or worse yet, what the author was told is the history of Taekwondo. There was very little if any reference to the historic records.

Being an amateur historian with a Bachelor's degree in the subject I felt that it only natural that I approach the work with real research. So it turned from a few page essay to a research thesis. While I ended up being proud of the finished project, the work yielded some interesting results. Many of peers and friends thought that I had gone too far.

My thesis also flew into the face of what so many of my instructors and peers had been told about the art they loved. They were used to the "mythology" of Taekwondo while I was giving a more real history. And the truth is, I think they preferred the mythology better. The simple forty-page thesis not only explained the history of Taekwondo, it explained to all my instructors and peers what kind of person I was. I'm a realists who despises "fantasyland".

That was back in 2013. I am no longer a formal practitioner of Taekwondo for reasons that will be explained later. But why then would I choose to dig up this work, add in a few extra thoughts, and put it on display? What purpose if any does the essay serve now? There is no real reason. However as an observation I will say that at the time I was writing the thesis, I was intentionally toning it down for the sake of the audience which I assumed would be a panel of Taekwondo instructors. But underneath the surface there was no hiding how I felt about the subject. Now that a wider audience can read the essay, the critical tone of my writing can show through without any concern.

- Matt Scott Diaz, 2018

Introduction

To this day I cannot tell anyone why. Why one day did I show up at a Taekwondo *dojang* (school)? It was late 2012 and I had amassed almost a quarter of a century experience in the martial arts. I had been a longtime student, researcher, competitor, fighter, and instructor. I never sold myself as some sort of "deadliest man alive" or an "ultimate bad ass", but I had made the martial arts a constant part of my life.

Back in 2012, I had studied numerous martial arts, achieved the coveted black belt status, had been a regional amateur Muay Thai tournament winner, went toe-to-toe with golden gloves champs in "smoker" boxing matches, been a reputable instructor of kids/adults, created program curriculums, had been certified as a Defensive Tactics instructor, survived street self-defense encounters, and had formal training in a number of different weapons disciplines. So why suddenly start over as a beginner and learn Taekwondo?

There's always been a drive inside of me to learn. The day I stop learning is the day I'm finally dead. There's a culture in the Asian-based martial arts to give the senior instructors with the most amount of years within the art the title of "master", "chief master", or even "grandmaster". However I've always believed that "mastery" is one of those things than we should strive for while knowing that we'll never achieve it. The only person on earth who ever had the right to consider themselves a "master" was Jesus of Nazareth. In keeping with this belief perhaps I felt it important to start over brand new as a novice in an art that I had no personal experience in. Perhaps I felt that I would keep with my desire of continuing to learn if I was able to humble myself to start a brand new endeavor and a brand new art.

So on January 2, 2013 I tied a white belt around my waist and lined up as a brand new student in the art of Taekwondo. In the area where I lived there were (at the time) five Taekwondo schools. My decision for picking the one I did had more to do with a close location and a returned call. But by that time I had already made up my mind that I would start this new journey.

A curious and critical mind

For the first few months it was all a little uncomfortable. In the realm of sparring, full-contact fighting, and in self-defense I had more experience than anyone at the school. I forced myself to be humble and just learn. But there was no denying that my patience was being tested by sitting in the beginning lessons hoping to actually learn something. Perhaps in my impatience, I jumped into researching the very art that I decided to practice.

There are no shortages of books on Taekwondo and I made it point to obtain an extensive library. Often looking for used lots sold on eBay, I had amassed a number of materials. Initially my reason for obtaining the material was to almost supplement my training. Because of my previous experience it wasn't difficult for me to learn material ahead of what my rank was. But while obtaining my collection of Taekwondo references, I took notice of something interesting.

The overwhelming majority of books on Taekwondo will devote the body of their work to the physical aspects usually accompanied with a number of photographs. But they will offer very little if any on the history and/or origins of the art of Taekwondo. Many of the books that will offer any sort of historical background on the art will be extremely brief and often times will be solely done for the purpose of self-promotion. There will be no historical documentation offered and will often appear as if they are simply recounting what the author(s) were already told.

Here's almost a summation of what many books on Taekwondo will offer as the history;

"Modern Taekwondo is the descendant of the noble martial arts as instructed to the warriors of ancient Korea hundreds of years ago. It stands as the pinnacle of martial arts training by combining modern athleticism and training with code of conduct to live by."

The first lesson in the study of history is to learn that history is not defined as the study of the past, it is the study of the *recorded* past. Yes historic records can be opened to interpretation and not all records are factual. But most of the practitioners of Taekwondo have never truly been taught a history of Taekwondo, but have been taught the mythology or folklore of Taekwondo. A few of these same practitioners would also set themselves up as experts on the origins of Taekwondo; but the truth is many of them are very ignorant of their own art.

Granted the above italics is my take on what would be a summation of what many Taekwondo authors expound. But as an amateur historian, a realists, and (God-forbid) an occasional cynic; whenever I hear words similar to my example, it makes me think that not all is at it seems. So early in my training with Taekwondo, I began to truly research the art known as Taekwondo. In many ways I was the perfect candidate to research the art's history. While I was an active practitioner at the time of my research, I was still an outsider. I had not been a practitioner for decades and it certainly was not my first art. Thus I could look at the subject with a critical mind while still having the first hand perspective as a longtime martial artists.

A fast rise

It didn't come as a surprise to both the other students as well as the instructors that I rose through the belt ranks at an alarmingly fast rate. I don't say that to be haughty and in truth it was solely due to my previous experience. The rapid rise allowed me to share my previous experience as an instructor in the school. Teaching both kids and adults was nothing new and I can certainly say that I brought a new perspective that I don't believe the students were expecting. The biggest element that I brought was a focus on the fighting elements of the martial arts. Under my programs, both the kids and adult sparring programs flourished. In addition I began promoting tournaments as well as coaching the students to compete.

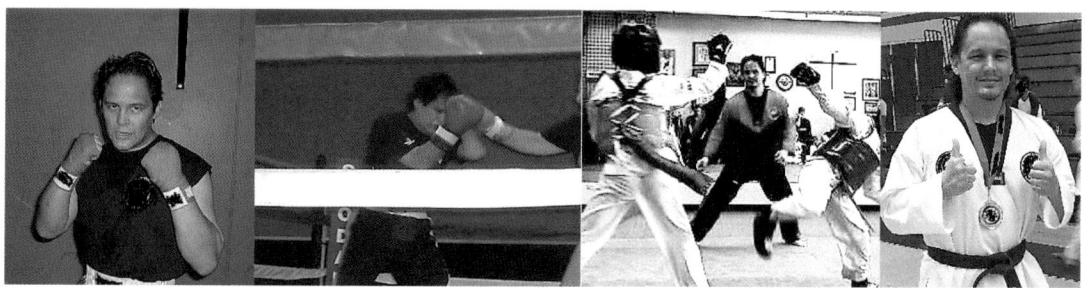

In a year I had gone from being a competitive brawler to a Taekwondo coach and finalist. This gave me a new perspective as I was now actively involved in the art that I was researching. (Photos by author)

Life has shown me that the instructor learns often as much as the students during teaching. Becoming a Taekwondo instructor allowed me to continue learning and gain a tremendous amount of personal satisfaction with teaching. But it also meant that I was becoming more dedicated to the art known as Taekwondo. I had started as an outsider but was now becoming a fully active participant.

In just over a year, I was soundly proficient in all the requirements for testing for the coveted black belt. As a longtime martial artists this was not something that I took lightly nor did I consider it to be an ultimate goal. But it was around this time that I made the decision to write my work on the history of Taekwondo. At the time I naturally had a degree of comradery not only with people at the dojang, but also the regional Taekwondo community. It was for this reason that I believe that I purposely toned down the critique of the art of Taekwondo in discussing the history. But there was no way that I was able to mask the fact that I had a real criticism for the modern history of Taekwondo. The truth was the history of Taekwondo was rife with controversy and scandal. Perhaps my expression of such offended some close to me as my essay was primarily received with a false sense of indifference.

A changing journey

After earning my first degree black belt, I continued my training. And it was around this time that my instructor expressed interest in having the school join an international Taekwondo organization. For the purpose of liability I won't mention the group by name nor any of the leaders and truthfully it doesn't matter. There are so many organizations just like them. Their goal is to persuade schools to join under their umbrella while they seek to garner favor with one of the big two organizations; either the International Taekwondo Federation (ITF) or the World Taekwondo Federation (WTF) which includes the Kukkiwon (the central dojang in Seoul, Korea). This particular group touted itself as a "world" organization with affiliate schools in South America, Canada, and in places like Israel.

Like all the other organizations, this one promised great things such as business support, curriculums, tournaments, and advertising but the cost was high. The organization not only wanted a charter fee and an annual fee, they also wanted a portion of the fees that were charged to the students as well as for every student to be an individual annual member of the organization as well. What they were really selling or giving in return was the same thing that just about all of these similar Taekwondo organization sell… the *illusion* of prestige.

As someone who earned his degree in history of modern Asia as well as being born to an Asian mother, I am wholly familiar with the concept of "never losing face". A vital component to Asian culture is the concept of not losing face. In essence not losing face means never suffering any sort of disgrace. Disgrace comes whenever your validity or prestige is questioned or flat out revoked. A common defense for avoiding disgrace is to set up some sort of system that offers hierarchy, order, structure, and prestige.

Asia has a long history of creating social and political systems that are never to be question. These systems (such as China's Confucian Class system or Japan's Feudal system) establish a sense of order and structure. The structure is to be followed to the letter and never questioned. Questioning causes chaos and disgrace. If some asked me what is the essence of Japan's code of the samurai (Bushido) I would argue it mandates that a warrior "never question". Never question your lord, your orders, or the way of things; no matter how unjust or wrong it could be! This culture idea has maintained itself today in Asian-based martial arts particularly in the leadership and organizations than oversee the arts. Taekwondo has been the worst when it comes attempting to control the art through the various organizations.

The school that I was training at would eventually be recruited into the aforementioned Taekwondo organization. This organization was essentially going to offer the school the illusion of prestige by being connected to them. The organization supposedly got their prestige with their connection to the Kukkiwon. I was naturally skeptical about the school joining the organization but it was not my decision to make at the time. I placed my criticism on the sideline and attempted to embrace the idea. The one thing that the organization did promote were sparring tournaments. As my body ached for the thrill of combat sports, I began competing. It had been years since my last Muay Thai or boxing fight but I put my former days aside and began fighting in the organization's tournaments eventually earning the bronze medal in their Grand National Championships.

After another year of dedication to Taekwondo where I would also become a co-owner at the school I trained at, it became time to earn my second degree black belt. My instructor at the time insisted that I test at the Grand National Championship where I was competing. A large group of the students and instructors made the long trip where we paid our entry fee and paid for the hotel room. At the time I was excited but in the end it was a big letdown. While I enjoyed competing and winning the bronze, the test itself was nothing but bloated pomp and circumstance without any essential core meaning. It was at this time that I was told not to turn in any thesis paper similar to this one for my second degree black belt. The essay for my second degree black belt test was not to be duplicated or even inspired by my (this) thesis for my first degree black belt. Any critique of Taekwondo or any organizations were to be stifled. The leaders of the organization (assuming they would even read it) would likely take offense to it. I did what I was told and instead fabricated a short essay.

That was when I was about to discover that my criticism had been right all along. Part of the history of Taekwondo has to do with all the various tyrannical organizations that sell prestige at a high price through the art. These organizations with their almost Mafioso methods are what generally causes the controversies and scandals attached to Taekwondo. I felt that my thesis on the history of Taekwondo was not only correct, it wasn't critical enough. At the time I was trying to be loyal and respectful to the art, the school I was training at, and maybe to the Taekwondo community. But maybe I should have made a stronger point.

The school that I once trained at and co-owned no longer exists. I had tried to warn the other instructors that things needed to change if the school was to survive. They didn't heed my warnings and insisted on a strategy that I knew would fail. Unfortunately I turned out to be correct. Thus I ended the Taekwondo journey at second degree black belt. But did it really matter? While I was sad to see the journey end, I cannot say that the art itself truly taught me something I didn't already know. But that's not to say that I didn't learn anything from the experience. I learned more about human behavior and social behavior through working in Taekwondo. Maybe the thesis that I wrote stands as the one tangible proof that I actually did learn something from Taekwondo.

So I present my original essay presented to the reader as some insights about Taekwondo… from an outsider's perspective.

The History of Taekwondo; an outsider's perspective

Taekwondo is not my first martial art. When I first stepped into a dojang as a prospective student, I had already been involved with martial arts for a quarter of century. I had played the role of competitor, researcher, instructor, and longtime student. And despite the fact that I honestly began my Taekwondo journey with a humble attitude, there is no denying that my previous experience gave me a unique perspective in my training. My personal history in the martial arts would aide my new endeavor into Taekwondo but it would also give me a unique perspective about the art itself as a new student.

As with any new endeavor, I have always made a point to personally research all the historic and cultural aspects first. For the sake of argument; if I was to become involved with flamenco dancing, I would make a point to personally study not only the history of flamenco music and dance, but also the history of 18th Century Spain as well as Castilian culture. As one who earned his Bachelor's degree in the study of history, I do consider myself an amateur historian. Thus it becomes vital to have an understanding in the historical foundation of any endeavor I decide to partake in. Taekwondo was no exception.

One of the first lessons in the study of history is to understand a core principle; history *is not* the study of the past. History is the study of the *recorded* past. It is the study of what people in antiquity took the time to write down. For example, a historical argument could be made that the Ancient Celtic people had no "history" prior to arrival of the Romans. That is not to say that the Ancient Celts had no past, no culture, and no folklore. But with no known written language; there was no history. Archeology, Anthropology, Sociology, and other academic studies can all study the past. But history is the study of what someone of the past recorded or wrote down or canonized for later generations. Given this, it must be understood that any record of the past need not necessarily be concerned with facts or truth; it is just discussing human events that someone took the time to write down. Each person that took the time to record the past may have his/her own personal motives in their telling of the events. An example would be the telling of an event during the American Civil War – one account as told by a "Billy Yank" Union soldier, the other from a "Johnny Reb" Confederate soldier. Both accounts would be understandably different despite the fact that they were both recording the same events. When understanding a historic perspective the reader of any history must try to understand first from what perspective is the author (historian) is coming from. What are the historian's motives behind the historic record and does their own personal experience affect the recording of his/her work?

My perspective in telling of the history of Taekwondo is essentially that of an outsider. I had not spent the last quarter of a century involved in arts, schools, or organizations that had anything to do with Taekwondo. But I had spent a number of decades training for long hours in just about everything that had to do with martial arts. Thus in examining the history of Taekwondo, my previous experience gave me elements to compare and contrast as well as a strong foundation in understanding what the martial arts in general were about and how the art of Taekwondo found a place in the combat arts. And more importantly, my unique experience meant that I would have no preconceived notions about the history of Taekwondo. I was neither a complete novice naïve to all aspects of the martial arts nor was a longtime practitioner in Taekwondo who was rigid in his understanding of the art. I began my research with a truly unique perspective.

The eye of the beholder

The history of Taekwondo is somewhat elusive at best. Upon researching Taekwondo, almost immediately I noticed the two part enigma in the history of the art. The first is that almost all leaders and pioneers of Taekwondo have a steadfast desire to trace the art to that of the ancient arts of the Korean warriors. This desire appears to be for the purpose of lineage and to give the art more prestige, something that is important to the Asian culture. Out of all the "classical" or "traditional" Asian-based martial arts, Taekwondo is in fact one of the youngest arts being a mere sixty years old which makes lineage vitally important. The second part of the enigma has been the discrepancy about the history of Taekwondo for those past sixty years. In researching the history of the art for the past decades, one can get a myriad of different histories that will conflict with each other. It will depend on which organization you are getting information from.

Most American Taekwondo dojangs have membership to a regional or national organization. That organization may have a connection to an international organization that oversees the overall curriculum, the rankings, and at least a small degree of management of the individual dojang. In addition, those organizations will have its official interpretation on the history of Taekwondo itself. Each organization's official history of Taekwondo may differ greatly primarily due to political reasons. A specific "official history" for one organization may provide political validation and provenance but only for that specific organization. Thus each organization may have a completely different "official history" of Taekwondo. The best example would be that of much documented rivalry between the International Taekwondo Federation (ITF) and the World Taekwondo Federation (WTF).

The official history of Taekwondo according to the ITF is centered on famed martial artist General Choi Hong Hi. Choi Hong Hi is said to have combined his studies of the indigenous Korean art of Taekkyon and his legitimate ranking in Shotokan Karate (from the founder Gichin Funakoshi) into a unique martial art. An art which in 1955 he called Taekwondo (which he spelled as Taekwon-do) under the approval of the various *kwans* (schools) who were meeting to unify the various arts and expand the cultural significance of the Korean people. However the WTF will have a different story.

According to the WTF which was founded in 1973, Choi plays a minimal role in the history of Taekwondo. Instead, Taekwondo is seen as simply a modern interpretation of the indigenous art Taekkyon, traced to the ancient warrior class of Korea, and developed under the newly formed WTF. The WTF refutes (for the most part) any connection to Japanese or Okinawan influences and any role that Choi played in the development and international spread of the art.

As stated previous, in attempting to explain the history of Taekwondo, my perspective is that of an outsider. Taekwondo is not my original art. I did not begin 25 years ago in Taekwondo as the sole art in my entire training nor have I spent my time under one large international Taekwondo organization which has only preached its own "official" history of Taekwondo. Thus as someone who began his training outside of Taekwondo, I can discuss the art's history without any preconceived notions or any partiality (for the most part).

I should also tell my readers that two decades ago when I immersed myself in other martial arts, I would hear about various historic or contemporary controversies occurring in the various Taekwondo institutions. Upon hearing about the various scandals I would sneer in an almost haughty manner at the time thinking of Taekwondo as the "amateur" or "beginners" martial art where a black belt was given so long as you paid a mere year of membership dues at the local strip mall dojang. Many of my peers felt the same way. Perhaps we were jealous of Taekwondo and its success. Perhaps like most human beings we falsely believed in our minds that could elevate ourselves by bringing others down. Perhaps we truly weren't acting like martial artists. Whatever the feeling at the time, I now know that it was misplaced.

And yet now at this moment, years later with some wisdom that comes from maturity and a number of long hours of research; I can provide some insights into the history of Taekwondo from the perspective of an experienced outsider. This outsider originally watched Taekwondo from afar for a number of years and originally had no interest in partaking of it. Years ago I never thought that would ever step inside a dojang; and now I have made the "Way of Kicking and Punching" a major part of my life.

Beginning the journey of research

The reader should allow me state that my area of study for my Bachelor's Degree in History was in modern Asia. Thus I have a solid historical background in the environment which Taekwondo was formed. I should also state that in my opinion it is important to discuss the history of Korea not in ancient times, but in the exact time period in which the art of Taekwondo was being developed. Many Taekwondo organizations may have their own unique theories on the history of the art. Many of these various organizations may offer discrepancies over who actually developed or founded the art of Taekwondo based on their own political structure and their current leadership. But despite their discrepancies, almost all of them attempt to trace a lineage of Taekwondo to arts practiced by Ancient Korean warriors which is not truly factual. The truth is most martial arts (as an art) are not really *founded*, but *codified*. What is also true is that there is virtually no real connection of Taekwondo to any ancient fighting art found in Korea. However the same can be said about any modern fighting art; there is almost no real lineage to anything in antiquity.

A statue of the Ancient Warrior Kumkang Yuksa in Korea linked to the warrior culture (A). Many Taekwondo practitioners and organizations attempt to establish a lineage of the ancient warriors of Korea (such as the *Hwarang*) to Taekwondo (B). But arguably this makes as much sense as trying to establish an exact lineage of the ancient boxers of Greece ("Thermae Boxer", National Museum of Rome (C)) to the modern sport of boxing (D). The connecting of an ancient lineage is generally only for the vain purpose of validating the prestige of an art. But prestige should come from the art's current practice – not its ancient "roots". All photos/images are public domain.

No single individual person can truly found an art that is completely unique, original, or separate. What they can found or create is a specific system, curriculum, and method of martial arts. Using General Choi for an example, even according to the ITF and his own biography Choi was a certified black belt in Shotokan Karate, formally trained in the art of Taekkyon, and had a military education. His art of Taekwondo became an almost perfect blend of all three disciplines. High powerful kicks and free-sparring practices with a training partner coupled with the structure curriculum and influence of *kata* (forms) of Shotokan in addition to military discipline. Thus his art of Taekwondo was greatly influenced on his own previous training and experience which is not unique. His teacher in Shotokan (Funakoshi) founded his art on his own previous training and experience with the Okinawan revivers of *Te*. In other words for illustrative purposes – someone can create a steerable axel, a steel belted radial tire, and a differential drive system. But no one can reinvent the concept of the wheel!

Every single solitary cultural civilization will have a standing military. That military will have a martial system specifically designed for military purposes. In order for that military to function, there will be some sort of code of conduct designed for strict discipline. The ancient Spartans learned the skill of the phalanx (battle formation) as well as ancient Greek weaponry and hand-to-hand combat. But they also learned specific codes of conduct codified in a number of mottos that they lived by one of the more famous being; "Son, return with your shield, or on it" (a motto of victory or death, nothing in-between). The modern United States Marine undergoes intense training in marksmanship with the 5.56mm M4 Carbine, CQC (Close-quarter Combat) and even the relatively new MCMAP (Marine Corps Martial Arts Program). They also live by their official motto of "Semper Fi" (short for Semper Fidelis, Latin "Always Faithful") and instill a honor and loyalty to God, County, Corps, Family, and Self (in that order) all of which is designed to instill intense discipline.

Every modern civilization with an extensive and rich cultural past will have some sort of military history in its early culture (A – An ancient Greek Hoplite, B – A Colonial Minuteman of America). But while those historic military groups serve an important cultural purpose for a sense of pride and lineage, in a practical sense they have almost nothing to do with any modern military applications (C – Greek Hellenic Special Forces, D – Modern United States Army Rangers). All images/photos are public domain.

The point being is that a combative system coupled with a mental training code of conduct is as old as time and is something that modern martial arts such as Taekwondo have no unique monopoly on. And arguably none of these combative systems can truly state that they were founded by a sole individual with a completely new, revolutionary, and unique skillset. They are in fact the culmination of centuries of evolution. What is unique about modern martial arts is the fact that they are not designed for the purpose of an established military program – but for civilian purposes. They are not necessarily designed for the soldier on the battlefield, but for the everyday person who may be called upon to use fighting skills for self-protection.

But even civilian based self-defense systems are not unique to Taekwondo or other Asian-based martial arts. In any civilization past or present with middle to upper class members of the culture, there will usually be some sort of system or systems of self-protection. The sophistication of the system will depend on outside variables. For example in both the Georgian-era (1714-1830) and Victorian-era (1837-1901) England, different systems of self-defense were born from bare-knuckle boxing, fencing, and quarterstaff to give the gentry class a method of protection from highwaymen and urban hooligans.

Above are examples of a rich history of civilian self-defense systems that were developed and flourished in the west. The left photos show the techniques of Edward William Barton-Wright of England. The last two photos show the work of American Prof. F.S. Lewis's book *The New Science of Weaponless Defense.* **Both systems included empty hand and weapons in their curriculum. All images are public domain.**

Many Taekwondo stylists and historians have an overwhelming need to trace a legitimate lineage of the art to the ancient fighting history of Korean such as the Hwarang warriors who were prevalent during the Silla Dynasty of Korea until the 10th Century. Despite the historic records of the Hwarang, we have no specific details of the techniques that they may have practiced. And whatever they may have practiced was relevant at that time and place. It has little to nothing to do with what is relevant to a 21st Century martial artist in the United States. It makes as much sense as trying to create an exact lineage of a modern boxer to the boxers of Ancient Greece. And arguably there exists more specific historic records of the exact techniques of the Ancient Greek Boxers than that of the Hwarang. Arguably the real purpose of tying the art of Taekwondo's lineage to the ancient Hwarang is to offer the art more cultural legitimacy and validity. But in my opinion the attempt is trivial at best.

That may sound harsh but the truth is (at least here in America) the average person who walks into the local dojang is not attempting to somehow be a part of a warrior tradition that existed in 10th century Korea. Any real validity and legitimacy for Taekwondo is found not in a false lineage to Korea's ancient history, but in any positive utilitarian purpose the students may find in its practice. It matters little what ancient culture miniscule affect might have had on a given martial art. What matters more is what that modern martial art is producing now…and who. There is more power in where we are now, not where we might have come from!

But to be fair, we should compare the art of Taekwondo to some of the historic indigenous arts of Korea. For the history of Korea, there are three primary indigenous arts that act as a starting point to discuss the influence of Korean culture on Taekwondo; *Subak*, *Taekkyon*, and *Ssireum*. There exist other ancient arts according to legend but these three are said to have had an influence on the art of Taekwondo – which they may very well have had even if minimal.

This image shows Silla dynasty warriors practicing the unarmed combat of Subak. Image is public domain.

Subak (sometimes spelled Soo Bahk) is stated to be the generic term for unarmed combat methods as practiced by ancient Korean military personnel. It's reasonable to assume that Subak (rough translation; "Hand Skill") is simply a word to describe the unarmed combat method portion that the ancient Korean military would practice much like the words "boxing" or "wrestling" referred to the unarmed portions of what the Ancient Greeks practice. Considering the fact that almost nothing is known about the specific details of Subak, we can also assume that it is not a specific discipline but a generic term to describe ancient Korean martial arts – something that almost every culture has. What we do know is that it was a sophisticated form of hand-to-hand combat for the warrior class and complimented the training of weapons and tactics. There is some evidence that Subak was also practice as a competition. The practice of Subak decreased in popularity around the late 14th Century when Neo-Confucianism stressed literary arts over martial arts. The historic record shows that Subak existed, but we don't have specific details of the art. Subak decreased again with the Japanese conquest of Korea and is not currently practiced in its original form.

Modern Taekwondo (A) and the traditional Taekkyon (B)

At first glance it may be easy to see a similarity between Taekwondo and Taekkyon, particularly with the use of high kicking techniques. But upon closer inspection, it becomes apparent that modern Taekwondo has a myriad of other adaptations in its development and it may share more similarities with other non-Korean arts than the indigenous Korean arts. (Photo A is public domain. Image B by author)

Taekkyon (roughly translated "kicking game" or "kick striking") is considered by some to be a decedent of Subak however Taekkyon is currently practiced as a cultural art in Korea and as a sport. At first glance the art has the appearance of a dance with no connection to karate, kung fu, or even Taekwondo – except in the fact that the art has all the flashy high kicks of modern Taekwondo as well as the practice of free sparring. The art was also known to be practice in competition styles between different villages. In many ways, Taekkyon stands as Korea's indigenous and continuous martial arts. For this reason, Taekkyon is sometimes said to be the ancient "root art" of modern Taekwondo. ITF's official history is that General Choi Hong Hi used his initial training of Taekkyon (including the kicks and the free sparring aspects) with the structure of his Shotokan Karate training to create the uniquely Korean art of Taekwondo and that he found inspiration from *Taekkyon* into the name of *Taekwon-do* because of their linguistic similarities. WTF's official history is that numerous Korean participants worked to modernize the art of Taekkyon and Subak into what is now the art of Taekwondo. But that's arguably where the similarities and connection ends. Modern Taekwondo has more in common with Japanese/Okinawan karate than with Taekkyon. In fact when the art was being introduced to the western world, Taekwondo was often referred to as "Korean Karate". While some saw this as demeaning to both the Koreans and karate itself, in many ways Taekwondo was seen as an expanded and improved Korean version of karate.

A modern Ssireum match held in Korea. Photo is public domain.

Like Taekkyon, Ssireum (roughly translated "to overcome") is an art indigenous to Korea and it is the country's folk wrestling tradition, something most cultures have. Like most folk wrestling traditions, it was often used to settle village disputes in a controlled competitive setting. Practiced in a circular sandpit, two combatants used grappling techniques to bring each other to the ground. It is still practiced today and believe it or not, it is actually the real national sport of Korea. Unlike Subak and Taekkyon, for the most part Ssireum has remain completely unchanged and has an intact lineage to its past. Many modern participants of Ssireum also compete in other combative sports including modern MMA.

Looking at these three indigenous arts, we actually see little influence on the development of Taekwondo (some exception with Taekkyon). The exact techniques of Subak are too unknown to make a direct connection, and there is little to no connect of Ssireum to Taekwondo. And even Taekkyon and Taekwondo only really share the high powerful kicking techniques and free sparring training – almost everything else has almost no connection. Taekkyon in both ancient and modern times was not practices in a dojang or hall but rather practiced outside in the village square complete with a whole uniform and footwear with no connection to the modern dobok uniform of today. The patterns (forms, hyungs, or poomsae) are completely different as they resemble a flowing dance rather than a precise combative series of techniques. There are also no belt grades in Taekkyon. So the questions becomes where exactly did modern Taekwondo get its current structure, curriculum, and discipline as they seem to share little with their indigenous predecessors. More importantly, what are the origins of Taekwondo?

Forged in the Fire

Rather than attempting in vain to draw a connection of Taekwondo to Ancient Korea, it is more important to draw a real connection of Taekwondo to the immediate history and political environment in which it was codified under. It matters little to know what the ancient warriors of Korea may have practiced in their martial arts tradition. What is more important is to understand the mindset of the men of the last century who would work tirelessly to codify, build, and expand the art that we now call Taekwondo. What did these pioneers intend for the art to become and in what political environment did they live in that may have shaped their dreams and goals? And what methods did they use to achieve these goals? To do that, we must first have a brief understanding of the history of what we now call South Korea; officially called the Republic of Korea.

The history (that is the official historic record) of the Republic of Korea only spans just under 70 years having been officially established in 1948. Its current leadership shares no exact lineage to any royal family or governmental dynasty. But in its short period of history, the country commonly known as South Korea has undergone some of the most internally and externally tumultuous times of almost any Asian nation. Once a subjugated territory of Imperial Japan, South Korea would only know its independence after World War II. Afterwards it would face a history of foreign military administration, an international war that would divide the country, six different official republics, two violent military coups, and a presidential assassination by a cabinet member. Not mention numerous bloodthirsty dictatorships, widespread corruption, and constant tensions with its neighbor to the north (North Korea; The Democratic People's Republic of Korea). It would be during these fiery times that Taekwondo would be forged. The result would be a martial art unlike any other because the circumstance in which it would be codified would be extremely unique.

A brief political history of South Korea (Republic of Korea) [Public Domain]

- **(1910-1945)** Imperial Japan occupies the entire Korean peninsula taking it by force (under the so-called 1910 Japan-Korea treaty) and ending the Korean Empire. During this time, the Korean people would be subjugated and the Korean culture itself suppressed including its indigenous martial arts would be outlawed. As a result, Japanese culture would influence Korea, even if by force.
- **(1945-1948)** The U.S. Military would act as administration for order. Japan's unconditional surrender would liberate Korea as the US maintains order and prevents Russian/Chinese communists' advisors in the North from influencing the South. Relative order is maintain, but Korea struggles to become a nation again.

- **(1948-1960)** The First Republic of Korea is formed. With US support, President Syngman Rhee would become the first president. This would establish the South as an independent nation and also end the possibility of the communists influence. The initial administration is seen by some a "puppet" administration that is corrupt.

- **(1950-1953)** The Korean War breaks out. Involving 6 nations and the newly formed United Nations it would test the first Republic as well as lead to the official border (the 38th Parallel) dividing North and South Korea. Tensions between the two would continue for years and even to this day.

- **(1960-1961)** The Second Republic of Korea is formed. A student revolt would exile President Rhee who would flee to Hawaii. Despite the successful revolt, the new republic would fail to maintain order or impose reforms and would ultimately fail, lasting only 8 months.

- **(1961-1963)** Military Coup de'etat establishes dictatorship. General Park Chung-hee would stage a military coup and completely transform the government and ushering in the Third Republic of Korea. The military coup would make a number of promises to the Korean people and the world, but would fail in most.

- **(1963-1972)** The Third Republic of Korea was established by General Park who became president. While economic growth would be seen under the Third Republic, it would usher in yet a fourth republic and Park's dictatorship.

- **(1972-1979)** The Fourth Republic of Korea would begin with Park suspending the standing Korean Constitution and declaring martial law. Later making himself President for life and creating an industrial dictatorship with a host of human rights violations. The republic and Park's tyranny would only end with Park's assassination by a member of his own cabinet.
- **(1979-1987)** The Fifth Republic of Korean also began with a military coup. Despite more economic growth, distrust of the government leads to wide protest and a call for more civil and human rights.

- **(1987-Present)** The Sixth Republic of Korea has lasted the longest out of all the republics with a number of reforms made and an equal number of high profile scandals. Ironically, the current President (at the time of this writing) is Park Geun-hye, the daughter of former general, president, and Dictator Park Chung-hee.

It is this recent history of South Korea that the art of Taekwondo can trace an exact real lineage to as well as a distinct influence that the history has over the art. Beginning first with the Japanese occupation and its influence on the Korean people to the struggle of South Korea to form and maintain a truly independent nation; the history of Taekwondo would share similar parallels with the history of South Korea.

Judo founder Jigoro Kano (left; public domain) greatly influenced all the modern Asian-based martial arts that we know today. (Right; photo by author)

Much like the history of South Korea, the first step in the development of Taekwondo would begin not with Korea, but with Japan. As the first Asian nation to embrace a modern evolution with the Meiji Period (or Meiji Restoration), Japan would transition their martial arts cultures from military arts practiced by the samurai class to originally a peacetime culture art. For example, kenjutsu ("the art of the sword") transition to kendo ("the way of the sword"). Shortly after this period would emerge the most influential figure in the history of modern martial art in my opinion, Judo founder Jigoro Kano (1860-1938). Kano's influence would spread far and wide such to a point that he would inadvertently affect the structure and overall philosophy of almost all modern Asian-based martial arts including Taekwondo.

Kano, an educator by trade who taught economics and political science, would transition his intense study of Japanese jujitsu into his own system of Judo (essentially from the "art of" gentleness to "the way" of gentleness). But in addition to formulating his own techniques from jujitsu to judo, Kano made a mass amount of changes to the structure and curriculum on how the martial arts were taught. Influenced greatly by American educator John Dewey as well as the education system that he worked in, Kano applied the structure of a university into the art of Judo. This gave rise to the concept that any acceptable student could enter the dojo for the purpose of educating themselves in the art of Judo. This included the aspect of showing respect to the teacher, senior students, and the especially to the school itself. Contrary to the myriad of myth associated with the colored belt ranks and the coveted black belt rank, it was Kano who was the first to include a belt system as a way of signifying a level of proficiency and he was the first to have the *dan* or grade system for levels of black belt. Kano was also the first to have all students and instructors change out of their street clothes and into a *gi* or uniform for practice. And finally, while not the first to do so, Kano stressed the concept that the students would practice Judo and gain more than just the physical aspects of training, but gain what he called a "moral education".

Judo founder Jigoro Kano (A) and Shotokan Karate founder Gichin Funakoshi (B). Despite the fact that neither men were ethnically Korean, they played an indirect role in the development of Taekwondo in the way it is structured and taught. Both images are public domain.

Go to any family-based martial art school anywhere in America and you will find some core concepts such as belt rank, respect of seniors/instructors, dan grades, uniforms, and some sort of code of conduct or mental/spiritual training; all of which Kano would be the one to formulate them into a common aspect of the martial arts. Kano's system of structuring the martial arts was so profound that it would end up greatly influencing almost all of the Okinawan Karate masters who were visiting Japan at the time. Some of the Okinawan masters were actually greatly opposed to Kano's concepts (such as belt ranks and uniforms) because it was something not traditionally done in their arts. However, because of the utilitarian use and effectiveness of Kano's concepts, they were eventually adopted and are now all a staple of all

Karate systems. It is some of these very same core concepts and principles that survive today. Often times these concepts and principles are the very things that draw modern American students into participation in the martial arts as opposed to just joining a "fight school". They aid in providing the school with a true discipline as well as an art form. And it is these concepts and principles that also exist in the art of Taekwondo.

An unfortunate piece of history in the martial arts also includes the period of Imperial Japan and the conquering of Japan's neighbors (something that Kano and a number of Japan's martial arts masters were vocally opposed to). In 1910, Japan officially annexed Korea as Japanese territory under the Japan – Korea treaty of 1910 (at gunpoint mind you). During this time, indigenous Korean martial arts were official banned from practice. Despite the ban, arts like Ssireum and Taekkyon were often practice in secret as folk arts or cultural competitions in more remote locations in Korea. Also during this time many of the later innovators of the modern Korean martial arts began to study in various universities in Japan – including studying Japanese martial arts. Ironically, despite the intense nationalism and violence during this time, most reports state that the one group that peacefully shared ideas despite their ethnic differences was the martial artists at the time. Almost all the revered Japanese martial artists at the time were very outspoken against Imperial Japan and their war crimes against other nations so they had little to no issue teaching non-Japanese.

One of the most prominent Okinawan teachers working in Japan at this time was Gichin Funakoshi (1868-1957). Born in and ethnically Okinawan, Funakoshi opened a dojo in Tokyo and would go to influence and spread his art across the world. Funakoshi, unlike some of his Okinawan contemporaries, adopted the belt ranking system first implemented by Kano. General Choi Hong Hi was a direct student of Funakoshi during his education in Japan eventually earning his second degree black belt (no easy task given the intense training at the time). Choi would undoubtedly use the overall structure of Shotokan Karate to formulate his own theories.

Given the official history of the ITF, it is easy to see the direct influence that Funakoshi would have on the indirect development of Taekwondo. Other Korean martial arts innovators would also be greatly influenced by other Japanese martial arts such as Won Kuk Lee (1907-2003) who was also a student of Funakoshi. And even others such as Hwang Kee (1914-2002; founder of Moo Duk Kwan and Tang Soo Do, one of the first schools in Korea) still found influence by learning karate and also learning kung fu while he was in Manchuria.

Ultimately one could ask how relevant is all this information to Taekwondo? I would argue that it is important to understand all the influences that went into the development in the art of Taekwondo. When an average American steps into the average dojang they are most likely looking to gain physical, mental, and perhaps even spiritual training that will give them the tools to better at least an element in their lives. We must understand that an element of that was the structure and curriculum put together by men like Kano and Funakoshi who would end up inspiring men like the original *kwans* (schools) of Korean that would help codify the art of

Taekwondo. The average American dojang will have a grading system, a uniform appearance, a reverence for the school, and a moral educational program that does need to pay some homage to the Japanese and Okinawan influences. These influences added a great deal of positive elements in the development of Taekwondo as well as many of the core values. If we are to consider ourselves as martial artists, is it not important to share the knowledge will all interested students? And likewise, should we not recognize all (not matter what their national origin) who helped inspire us?

The infamous day on April 11th, 1955

Anyone can "Google" the date April 11, 1955 and without including the text "Taekwondo" will hit a number of websites that refer to the infamous day in the art's history. These various websites will have connections with various organizations including but not limited to the ITF, the ATA, and the WTF (to a lesser degree). Everyone who is a student of the history of Taekwondo will know of that specific date in history. But there will be disagreements on what exactly happened on that day and more specifically who would actually set the stage to conceive the art of Taekwondo. In short, everyone in Taekwondo will admit that the April 11th, 1955 date was a vital one to Taekwondo's history, but many will debate what exactly happened that day. The date is vital to the history of Taekwondo because it would involve the development and codification of the art itself. Most agree that prior to that date in history; Taekwondo would be a martial art without even a name much less an exact curriculum. Despite the immense disagreement on what occurred on that April 11th day, Taekwondo would at the very least finally become an art with a name. But who exactly would be the one to actually give Taekwondo its name? Was the name created by one person or by an entire panel of men who represented the 9 Kwans (schools) that existed at that time?

What everyone can agree on is a period of history immediately after Japan's surrender in World War II on September 2nd, 1945. The Korean people were liberated as a Japanese colony with the unconditional surrender, but that was hardly the end of Korea's hostile history. The victorious Allied Forces failure to balance control of the Korea with recognizing the sovereignty of Korean people along with the tyrannical yet growing communists forces in China and Russia would eventually lead to the Korean war, the Korean Armistice Agreements, and the 38th Parallel (South and North Korea). During this time Korea (in particular South Korea) would struggle to become a nation once again. And also during these chaotic times, any remnants of the indigenous Korean martial arts would struggle with their very existence. The art of Taekwondo would also struggle to evolve into a codified and legitimate martial art that was uniquely Korean. During this time, the art was poised to become a living symbol of Korean history and culture that could be shared with the world. Taekwondo would become a martial art unlike any other because it was founded under the most unusual circumstance.

General Choi Hong Hi is almost at the very center of Taekwondo and its rich and controversial history. To some he is the very father of Taekwondo, to others he is to be completely purged from all history books on both Taekwondo and Korean history, and some will claim that he should be considered somewhere in the middle. All photos are public domain.

Almost immediately after Japan's surrender, Korean martial artists were free to teach and open their own martial arts schools (called kwans) and a number of various kwans opened up with their own unique styles, forms, names, and curriculums. Under almost any other period in history, these different kwans would have been allowed to grow and flourish separately on their own without any interference. But as Korea was just ending decades of tyrannical rule under the Japanese and was now facing new turmoil, the importance of unification of all the kwans into one solid and uniquely Korean martial art became paramount. The nation of South Korea needed a unified cultural art form to call its own including a new universal martial arts that represented its history and culture.

The General

Choi Hong Hi was one of the founding members of the South Korean Army almost immediately after the surrender of Japan. He had founded his own kwan (Oh Do Kwan; "School of My Way") and used it to train the recruits of the newly formed South Korean Army.

According to most sources, Choi summoned the board that was to meet on April 11th, 1955. Other sources state that then President Syngman Rhee was the one that actually ordered the meeting of the board but even then, Choi was to be the one to carry out the meeting. This board was made up politicians, historians, and at least five original kwan masters (a total of 9 kwans are said to ultimately have an influence on the founding of Taekwondo). The purpose of this board was in fact to unify all the various styles and schools into one art and system. All existing documentation shows that Choi was the one who actually summited the name "Taekwondo", a name that was generally accepted due to the close resemblance to the indigenous art of Taekkyon and more importantly it eliminated the various other names that the different kwans were using such as Kwon Bup, Tae Soo Do, Gong Soo, etc.

This can be a point of extreme contention for some Taekwondo practitioners and historians. If Choi is given credit with being the first to coin the term *Taekwondo* (later he would spell it in English; *Taekwon-do)* as well as being the first to organize and initially develop the art, it elevates him more than just that of a pioneering martial artist to being the actual founder of Taekwondo. To some, Choi *is* the founder of Taekwondo and those later organizations are simply offshoots of his work. To others, Choi is merely *one of many* who helped develop Taekwondo but should not be seen as a founder. And yet still others discredit any of his involvement in Taekwondo at all.

In 1959, four years later after the April 11th meeting, the Korean Taekwondo Association (KTA) was formed with Choi as the first president. Undoubtedly Choi had a tremendous influence in the worldwide growth of Taekwondo in the early sixties. But it would be in the late sixties and early seventies that the historical records would begin to become confusing.

There are a number of stories surrounding Choi's early life that almost comes off as fantastic legends. But it is more important to focus on the elements of his life that can be verified, particularly those elements that also involve Taekwondo. He was born on November 9th, 1918 in the Myong Chun District in what was then Japanese controlled Korea (now North Korea). He was reportedly a longtime student of the indigenous Korean martial art of Taekkyon before leaving for Japan. While in Japan he would study English, mathematics, and economics. Choi would also study Shotokan Karate under a number of instructors including founder Gichin Funakoshi eventually earning his second degree black belt.

With the outbreak of World War II, Choi was forced to enlist in Japan's army but was later implicated in a Korean rebellion and was imprisoned. While imprisoned, it was said that he began teaching both fellow prisoners and guards. Upon the surrender of Japan Choi returned to Korea where he would become one of the founders of the South Korean military. Beginning as a second lieutenant in 1946, Choi would rise through the ranks over the next two decades, eventually reaching the rank of Major General in 1954. Choi would use the South Korean military to help promote his version of Taekwondo as both a fighting art and disciplined philosophy for the soldiers of the army. During this time, he would also find success as the premier mover in Korean martial arts having been a part of the April 11th board and in the naming of Taekwondo as well as becoming the first president of the Korean Taekwondo Association.

Choi Hong Hi around the time he would be promoted to Brigadier General (1952) and prior to the infamous day on April 11th, 1955 when Taekwondo would be first given its name. Photo is Public Domain.

Then President of South Korea Dr. Syngman Rhee (in office 1948-1960) would support General Choi and Choi's vision for Taekwondo by having the soldiers of South Korea learn Choi's version of Taekwondo. It is also said that President Rhee would be the one who actually ordered the unification of all the martial arts practiced in Korea thus leading to the meeting of the kwans on April 11th, 1955.

Even Choi's detractors have difficulty denying his success in early South Korean politics, the growth of new military, and the initial spread of the art of Taekwondo across the globe. His supporters point to the fact that he had been the first to station competent instructors across the world and would make it his mission to spread the art all across the globe. In 1965 he would author the first English language book on the complete curriculum. The following year he would found the International Taekwondo Federation. However it is interesting to note that even prior to these events in the mid-sixties, Choi would become unavoidable entangled in a number of the political hostility common found in newly formed nations. These political hostilities would have an effect on the art of Taekwondo as well.

South Korea after the Korean War would endure constant turmoil including going through three different Republics and eventually a military coup that resulted in the infamous Park Chung-hee's rise to power as President for Life. According to an interview given by Choi to Taekwondo Times by Dr. Kimm from 1998-99 (via www.tkdweb.nl), Choi had in fact participated in the coup but never believed that Park (a general at the time) would take over the Presidency and had originally promise to returned to the army once stability was obtain in South Korea. Choi would later become an outspoken opponent against President Park. Park and his supporters would retaliate against Choi politically by forcing him to retiring from the military and appointing him as the ambassador to Malaysia. According to Choi, President Park's later regime would create a hostile political climate that forced him into self-exile himself to Canada in 1972 to avoid being imprisoned as well as continue his work in the spread of Taekwondo.

Choi stated that he chose Canada as a more neutral western nation that would allow him to grow the ITF. He would live in Toronto until he had discovered that his cancer was inoperable. In a desire to be buried near his home land Choi returned to Pyongyang, North Korea where he died in 2002 at age 83. Like many organizations, the ITF would find it difficult to run smoothly without its established "father". Currently three different organizations all claim to be the leaders in the ITF with headquarters in Canada, Austria, and North Korea. Despite the rift in the ITF, Choi's style of Taekwondo is practiced internationally across the world with strong dominance in Canada, the UK, Eastern Europe, and North Korea and with good presence in most countries. In recent years there has been an attempt to unite the splinted ITF in recent years with some mild success.

(A) President Syngman Rhee (First President of South Korean) (B) President Park Chung-hee (President of the 3rd Korean Republic, later President for life, 4th Korean Republic). Photos are public domain. Both men would be inadvertently instrumental in the development of Taekwondo. Rhee would be the one to push for a unification of the Korean martial arts and promote the rise of Choi Hong Hi. Park would eventually cause Choi's self-exile and help usher in the rise of the World Taekwondo Federation.

"Government" Taekwondo

In 1973 the World Taekwondo Federation was founded and right or wrong it would take the art of Taekwondo in a different direction. It's important to understand what was going on in the nation of South Korea at the time. Two men who possibly inadvertently influenced the development and the very history of Taekwondo were President Dr. Syngman Rhee and President Park Chung-hee. Both men are praised by some historians and condemned by others. Both men had successes that in the lives as wells as controversies that haunted their legacies.

(A) General Douglas MacArthur and President Rhee   (B) General Park (right) who later became President

The history of South Korea after World War II is ripe with turmoil as the nation has struggled with foreign military administrations, two military coups/dictatorship, six different Republics, a presidential assassination, domestic revolutions, and mass political corruption not to mention the Korean War and tensions with North Korea. The art of Taekwondo would develop and grow under these tumultuous times, unique to just about any other martial art in the world. Both photos are public domain

Rhee (1875-1965) became the first president of the Provisional Government of the Republic of Korean and later the president of South Korea (or the First Republic). Over his three terms of office from 1948-1960, he would personally take Korea through its post-independence from Japan and through the Korean War. A staunch anti-communists Rhee would garner support from western nations such as the United States. He would also personally support General Choi and is said that he actually first ordered the unification of the Korean martial arts. It is often assumed that since many of the original kwans were technically civilian schools, Rhee lent his political support to the Oh Do Kwan (General Choi's school) since it was a military kwan used to train soldiers. Thus perhaps Choi owes a least some of his initial success to Rhee as well as development of Taekwondo. Rhee would slowly fall from power as discontent from the public increased and foreign aid from the United States decreased. It was often believed that many of his elections were rigged, but when elections were held for Rhee's running mate were found to have an almost impossible margin, it practically confirmed fraud in the voting. This led to the "April Revolution" which forced Rhee's resignation and his exile to Hawaii where he would live until his death. After his exile, Korea would move into what is now called the Second Republic of Korea which was short lived due to the lack of any stability lasting only eight months.

After the failed Second Republic of Korea, General Park Chung-hee would lead a military coup in 1961. According to the aforementioned interview with Choi Hong Hi, Choi was part of the coup after believing that the Second Korean Republic was too chaotic and that order had to be restored. Also according to Choi, he was under the belief that Park (then a General) was going to establish order then return to the army. Instead Park established himself as acting President (with the powers of a dictator), later to be officially elected as the President of the Third Korean Republic two years later. It would be Park who would later consider Choi a traitor due to his attempted alliance with North Korea and initiate Choi's self-exile.

During his first term as president, Park oversaw some of the major tensions between North and South Korea. A year after 1971 re-election, Park suspended the established constitution, declared martial law under the guise of a pending emergency with North Korea, and ushered a Fourth Republic of Korea. From that point on, Park was for all purposes a legal dictator of an autocracy and ushered in a tyrannical reign.

Park's economic policy did have some success in developing South Korea's struggling economy and his foreign policy succeeded for the most part in keeping North Korea at bay. But there can be little doubt that his presidency after 1971 was marred in total domination and numerous human right violations. Certainly he created an atmosphere where almost every element of Korean life and culture in South Korea was controlled and/or directly influenced by Park and the central government of South Korea. And it was during this time and in this atmosphere that some vital Taekwondo institutions would be born.

The Seoul Headquarters and the Olympic entity

Imagine a modest dojang in a small town in the United States. This dojang has an average student body filled with both adults and children alike. Now let's imagine this modest dojang pays a charter membership to a larger organization. There's nothing unusual about a martial arts school of any style paying some sort of homage and membership to a larger entity. In this day and age it becomes less and less that a martial art school remain completely independent. A membership to a larger organization allows for the school to have additional support, more advertising, business connections, and a degree of validation or recognition. But what if this particular dojang is a charter member of an organization with official ties to a central foreign government? What if this small American dojang holds accreditation with a central organization that is governed by a departmental ministry of the foreign government? What if this dojang was a member of both the WTF (the World Taekwondo Federation) and accredited with the *Kukkiwon*? That is what would make the dojang unique – not necessarily better, but unique in that its membership brings the dojang into a large global circle that is unlike any other.

Formed in 1973, the World Taekwondo Federation was designed to expand on the original KTA (Korean Taekwondo Association) as well possibly discredit the ITF (International Taekwondo Federation). At the time of the founding of the WTF, Choi Hong Hi had recently placed himself in self-exile. President Park ushered in the Fourth Korean Republic and had suspended the Korean Constitution. And the ITF had independently grown for the past seven years. From a political standpoint in the martial arts, it was not good for public relations if a former four-star general (Choi) and "founder" and innovator of a growing popular worldwide martial art was now in exile from the very nation and government that he had helped build.

Currently the number one function of the WTF (and is in fact part of its mission statement) is to promote, expand, improve the worldwide practice of Taekwondo as a sport both in regional tournaments, national tournaments, and international tournament as well as the Olympic games. The WTF is an official member of the Association of Summer Olympic International Federations. Certainly that alone would set the WTF apart from most any martial arts organization in their international scope and influence. Most martial arts organizations in the U.S. are generally regional or national and certainly have no connection with the Olympic committee. But what perhaps makes the WTF the most unique than any other martial arts organization is its political connection and inter-relations to the original KTA Central Dojang – later called the Kukkiwon.

The Kukkiwon is based in Seoul, South Korea and is known as the official World Taekwondo Headquarters as well as the home to the tournament division which what essentially is the WTF. The Kukkiwon is also responsible for the certification worldwide of all official instructors and black belt *dan* (degree) candidates. What makes this unique among just about all martial arts organization is that the Kukkiwon was established by and in fact is part of the South Korean government.

Almost all international martial arts organizations are essentially private groups. Run by a committee or board of directors, most international organizations are not even remotely funded or recognized by any country's government and are certainly not overseen by a government department. While it is true that some combative or martial arts tournaments may have to obey local laws pertaining to sanctioned matches (such as a local boxing match complying with a state's athletic commission), the promoter or organization needs only to be in compliance with local laws and allow government officials to witness the events. The government department has no control on how the organization is run.

While there is little detailed information about the connection between the WTF, the Kukkiwon, and Presidential Dictator Park Chung-hee, there exist no doubt that they all shared a connection. In the government-controlled dictatorship that Park created in Korea, both the WTF and the Kukkiwon flourished under similar styles of centralized control. It was Park who declared Taekwondo as the national sport of South Korea and allocated the funding to build the Kukkiwon. In addition, the newly elected president of the KTA (in 1971) Dr. Kim Un-Yong who would later head both the WTF and the Kukkiwon was once a powerful member of Park's cabinet having served as the Deputy Chief of the Presidential Protective Forces. Most certainly, the WTF and the Kukkiwon could not have even existed without Park's specific approval and more likely he had some influence in how both entities were formed.

It can also be argued that while not the primary goal of the Kukkiwon and WTF, a secondary goal could have been to discredit both Choi and the ITF. Park himself would use Choi's desire to spread Taekwondo to North Korea as traitorous to the people and government of South Korea obviously in an effort to discredit Choi. At the time, there could be nothing more treacherous to South Korea than to have any ties to North Korea. Choi always insisted that he was not acting with political motivations when he wanted to spread Taekwondo to North Korea – but there is no doubt that Choi was willing to attempt an alliance. More importantly, the damage had been done and Park had arguably sent his message to Choi.

The WTF and the Kukkiwon succeeded in truly unifying Taekwondo in South Korea as well as truly establish it as both a demonstration (A) and competitive (B) tournament art. The new leadership, with the financial and political support of the South Korean government, also would help spread the art arguably beyond what Choi and the ITF was able to do. Both photos are public domain.

While the WTF is not officially a department in the South Korean government and is run by a general assembly, it has a well-established connection to the Kukkiwon which is technically an entity of the South Korean government, overseen by the South Korean Ministry of Culture, Sports, and Tourism. It is also true that most of the ranking leaders in the WTF began a career in Korean and/or other Public Service prior to their work in the WTF. In fact, the inaugural tournament of the WTF was held at the Kukkiwon and there is some debate on how much influence and control the South Korean government has over the WTF and every school across the globe that is a charter member.

Most American Taekwondo practitioners whose dojang is affiliated with the WTF and the Kukkiwon, more often think very little of being part of an entity that has official ties to a foreign government. And it is doubtful that they give any additional thought to the notion that both the WTF and the Kukkiwon were founded and supported during the administrational reign of a South Korean dictator (Park) who had an established history of massive human rights violations against the South Korean people. It is reasonable to ask how one can honestly practice a moral education inside a dojang with ties to an entity with an established record of immorality.

Olympic/WTF style Taekwondo would make huge steps in popularity and influence under the leadership of Dr. Kim Un-Yong, but his leadership would also haunt the world of Taekwondo later. (Public domain image)

The "New" leader of Taekwondo

It has been said that if Choi Hong Hi created the traditional aspects and art of Taekwondo, Dr. Kim Un-Yong created the modern art of Taekwondo. Kim was actually not a martial artist at the time he took the role as President of the KTA and had a long history as a powerful public servant in the South Korean Government. His last position in the South Korean Government prior to taking the role of President of the KTA was the Deputy Director of the Presidential Protective Forces and he obviously had close ties with then president Park Chung-hee. From 1971 to 2004, Kim would serve various high-ranking positions of power in the KTA, the WTF, the Kukkiwon, and the International Olympic Committee (IOC) and he would help mold much of what we consider Taekwondo to this day.

What few people can argue is that prior to Kim Un-Yong, Taekwondo was never truly united and there was countless infighting and attempts to change or breakaway from early Taekwondo leadership. Even under Choi Hong Hi's leadership with his staunch beliefs and strong control, many of the various kwans fought with each other over control. At one point while Choi was traveling abroad spreading the art of Taekwondo, he had returned to find that there had been an effort to change the name of the art to *Tae Soo Do*. Kim, with backing from President Park, would completely reform the KTA and finally and officially unite the nine kwans under one banner and one art of Taekwondo. He would also be the first to put into a plan to create a central dojang which would eventually become the Kukkiwon approved and funded by President Park and the South Korean Government.

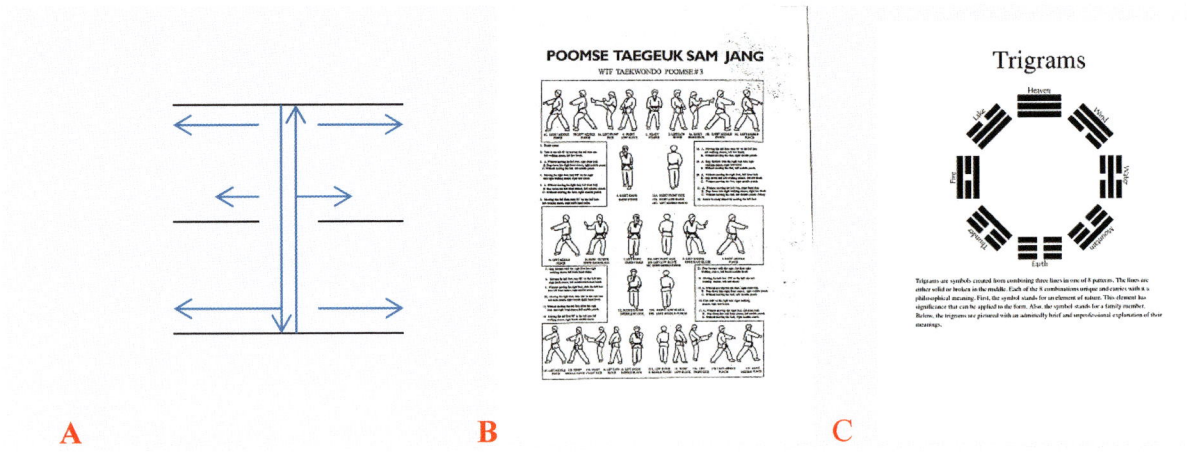

A   B   C

One of the first acts of the WTF was to change the pre-arranged patterns (poomsae) to contrasts with the ITF Chang Hon Forms created by Choi. What they came up with was two sets of forms based on the Chinese Trigrams (C) based on the classic works of the I-Ching. For example; Taegeuk 3 (B) follows the pattern of Ri (A) Fire and Sun. The last two images are public domain.

Out of the KTA and the Kukkiwon, the World Taekwondo Federation would be born with a goal to establish Taekwondo as the national sport of Korea as well as spread the art of Taekwondo. But an obvious question would be; would the art be the same as the one taught prior to the WTF? To begin with, under Kim, committees would be formed to change some of the key curriculums of Taekwondo. Prior to the WTF, the hyungs or poomsae (pre-arranged forms or patterns) would primarily be those taught by Choi called the Chang-Han forms (literally "Blue Cottage" Korean; Choi's pen name). Choi had developed them with many of his senior students as a representation of Korean history giving each form the name representing important persons or institutions vital to Korean history and culture. For example, one form is titled "Won-Hyo" named after the monk who first codified Buddhists teachings in Korea. And yet at the same time, the overall look and techniques of the forms were undoubtedly influenced by Choi's previous Shotokan Karate training. Even many of the other kwans outside of Choi's influence practices their own forms that were greatly or at least largely influenced by the forms of Karate.

The lighting of the Olympic Torch at the 1988 Summer Olympics in Seoul, Korea where Taekwondo would make its debut as a demonstration sport for the first time. That year's games would see some major controversies and scandals including the controversial loss of legendary boxer Roy Jones Jr. to Korean Park Si-Hun and Canadian 100 meter sprinter Ben Johnson who was stripped of his gold medal when he tested positive for steroids. The rise of Taekwondo to the Olympics would be equally marred with controversy and scandals. Image is Public Domain.

In the WTF's quest to establish Taekwondo as Korea's premiere art, committees were held to create new forms that better represented Taekwondo as a uniquely Korean art, separate from any Japanese martial arts. The result was the *Palgwe* forms, later replaced by the *Taegeuk* forms. Both sets include a total of eight forms based on the Chinese trigrams found in the *I-Ching* ("Book of Changes", one of China's oldest classical texts, traditional said to be the work of Confucius). The universally used *Taegeuk* forms primarily represented the sports elements of Taekwondo that was the being promoted under the WTF. Ironically, with the goal of attempting to remove the "Japanese" elements of Taekwondo and promote Korean culture in the art, the Taegeuk forms appear to represent more Chinese culture and elements. In addition, while forms and patterns are paramount in the training of most Asian-based martial arts, the Taegeuk forms became secondary or almost a mere formality art of the WTF's new Taekwondo.

One criticism against both the Palgwe and Taegeuk forms from both ITF Taekwondo practitioners as well as other Okinawan and Japanese martial arts practitioners is that the forms appear to be hastily put together strictly for the purpose of separating themselves from the ITF as wells as to distance Taekwondo from its Japanese/Okinawan roots. Whatever the reason, they remain an institution in the WTF curriculum.

It's important to note once again that during this period, Taekwondo as an organization was at a crossroads. Choi had already formed the ITF five years prior and had begun his self-exile due to his fear for his freedom and safety from President Park. For the KTA, the WTF, and the Kukkiwon all functioning under new leadership, it became important for them to discredit Choi Hong Hi or at the very least usurp him. Choi had been a four-star general recently self-exiled. He had also been a pioneer in the spread of Taekwondo across the globe and many students outside of Korea looked to Choi as founder of the art itself. If the government of South Korea was going to reclaim the art of Taekwondo, it would have to undermine Choi and the ITF. It would also have to have complete control over the art and the direction that it was to go. Thus began the long feud between the ITF and the WTF. It was essentially a feud between the independent work of Choi and his followers versus the government of South Korea's new Taekwondo organizations.

Above is a rough image of Kim Un-Yong towards the end of his career. At one time he was Vice-President of the International Olympic Committee, the President of the WTF/KTA, the founder of the Kukkiwon, and a member of South Korea's Assembly. But numerous scandals followed by investigations of bribery, embezzlement, and fraud at the height of his power would lead to his conviction and a prison sentence and ultimately his downfall. Image constructed by the author.

After truly unifying Taekwondo in Korea and changing the structure of Taekwondo and the manner in how it was controlled, Kim Un-Yong's next goal was to truly promote Taekwondo on the international stage. It arguably was clear that the method that he would eventually use to accomplish this task was to make the art an Olympic sport. It was not necessarily a new idea since Choi had earlier attempted to get his Taekwondo art to become an Olympic game as well.

Kim's tireless work would eventually lead to the art becoming a part of the 1988 Olympic Games in Seoul Korea as a demonstration sport. It would continue as a demonstration sport in the following 1992 games in Barcelona, Spain (there would be no demonstration sports in 1996 Atlanta games), finally become a full-medal sport in the 2000 Summer Olympic games in Sydney, Australia. It has remained a full-medal sport ever since (as of this writing). There can be little doubt in the unification, codification, and international growth of Taekwondo in the last decades of the 20th Century. And there is also little doubt that the success of Taekwondo can be greatly attributed to Kim and his leadership in the KTA, the WTF, and the Kukkiwon. But like most of some of the premiere leaders of Taekwondo, Kim would not escape controversy.

Kim would be implicated in the vote-buying scandal in Salt Lake City, Utah in the late 90's. At the time he was a member of the IOC and had apparently been part of the bribery scandal in an attempt to bring the 2000 Olympics to Salt Lake City, basically being paid with favors and gifts for his vote. The scandal ruined any chances he might have had to become President of the IOC in 2001, a position he was vying for in the hopes of using it to further Taekwondo. There would be later investigations in financial misgivings in his posts as both the leader of the WTF and his membership of the IOC. The corruption was sufficient enough to force his resignation of the President of the WTF in 2004.

But it did not end there as South Korean investigators built a case for bribery, embezzlement, and corruption when they uncovered about 5 million dollars in gold, diamonds, gems, and foreign currency inside his home. As much as he gave to the art of Taekwondo, a court showed that he illegally profited from the art of Taekwondo by stealing from it. Kim was convicted and served prison time. Many of his associates, aides, and a number of ranking members in the WTF were also implicated in various corruption scandals which led to their demise. There are some Taekwondo practitioners who still support Kim for his work in promoting the art for three decades, but the scandals still ended his career as a prominent leader in Taekwondo. Currently there is completely new leadership in the Kukkiwon, the WTF, and Olympic Taekwondo and a number of much needed reforms were made if for no other reason than to salvage the image of Taekwondo itself.

Pre-unifications and breakaway Taekwondo

Occasionally American martial artists will come across the unique entity of a "pre-unification" Korean art. That is to say an art with Korean origins somehow avoided the attempt by both Choi Hong Hi and Kim Un-Yong to unify with the various kwans into one Taekwondo style. For illustrative purposes, the best and most popular example of this would be the art of Tang Soo Do ("Way of the Chinese Hand). Primarily linked to famed Korean martial artists Hwang Kee (1914-2002) who founded the equally famed Moo Duk Kwan ("School of Martial Virtue"); initially Tang Soo Do was one of the few arts to open refuse to take part in the unification. According to most reports, Hwang Kee himself refused to take part in the unification due to his belief that Choi and the KTA sought to take over and control his organization. Both Kee and the Moo Duk Kwan had found initial success with the spread of Tang Soo Do across the globe and it helped greatly for overseas growth that American martial artists turned actor Chuck Norris was originally a Tang Soo Do practitioner.

It's also been said that it was because of Hwang Kee and the Moo Duk Kwan School that most of the training and techniques of Taekwondo actually flourished and some have gone so far as to state that the Moo Duk Kwan is what truly formed the art that we now call Taekwondo. Whatever the true origins are, due to the Moo Duk Kwan's refusal to fully unify and some of the failed early attempts to join the KTA, the art of Tang Soo Do was allowed to grow on its own without (for the most part) the political infighting and scandals that plagued Taekwondo. Kee would later rename his organization as Soo Bahk Do (a reference to the ancient and elusive indigenous art of Korea). In 1995, on the 50th Anniversary of the founding of Moo Duk Kwan, Hwang Kee officially changed the art's name from Tang Soo Do to Soo Bahk Do Moo Duk Kwan. The art has numerous practitioners worldwide and even the WTF officially recognizes Moo Duk Kwan as one of the nine founding kwans and it has close political relationship with the WTF and the KTA.

What is also peculiar in the industry of Taekwondo is some of the various private organizations that have broken away from either the ITF or WTF. One of the most popular especially in the United States is the American Taekwondo Association (ATA). According to the official history of the ATA (www.ataoline.com/history), the organization was founded by Haeng Ung Lee (1936-2000) in 1969 in Omaha, Nebraska.

Haeng was born in Japanese controlled Manchuria and began training in Korean martial arts at age 17. The ATA maintains that at least for a short period of time, Haeng was even a student under Choi Hong Hi. Haeng would begin teaching all over South Korea and at one point taught near a U.S. Air Force Base where he met ATA co-founder Richard Reed. In the early sixties, Haeng was sponsored by Reed to emigrate to the U.S. where they would found the ATA. In 1977, the ATA was moved to Little Rock, Arkansas where it remains today. In 1984, the ATA's style of Taekwondo would grow to a level where Haeng would found the Songahm Taekwondo Federation (STF; Songahm "Pine Tree") in an event to bring his art outside of the U.S. Haeng and his supporters found a degree of success in spreading their version of Taekwondo across the United States and later across the globe. Upon his death from cancer in 2000, the ATA council began referring to Haeng as "The Eternal Grandmaster".

Like the ITF, the ATA is not recognized by either the Kukkiwon or the government of South Korea. However the ATA does not appear to seek any recognition from either entity. Instead the ATA seems more interested in maintaining complete control over its organization as well as complete independence from any other Taekwondo organizations. They have complete copyright and registered trademark over their entire curriculum, logos, and even their equipment. They host various tournaments that are closed to any outsiders. And they have a complex system for certifying and recording their own belt ranks and their certified instructors. There exists other private Taekwondo organizations like the ATA, but the ATA is unique in its ability to grow and spread across the U.S. and the world completely independent from the political struggles that occurred in South Korea.

The purpose for mentioning both the arts of Tang Soo Do/Soo Bahk Do and the organization of the ATA for this work, is to illustrate the growth of Taekwondo/Korean based martial arts outside of the political turmoil that was occurring in South Korea with the KTA, the ITF, and the WTF along with the political turmoil that was taking place in the government of South Korea itself. It can be easily argued that some independent Taekwondo groups sought to remove themselves from the infighting. Both groups (as well as others that could be mentioned) found unique ways to spread the art of Taekwondo as well as the martial arts philosophy without taking part in the cut-throat politics.

However this does bring up another question; in this ability to remove themselves from the major politics of Taekwondo, did they end up creating something completely different? Is the Taekwondo that is practices under the ATA truly "Taekwondo"? Or for that matter, since the ITF is not recognized by the Kukkiwon and the South Korean government, is what they teach truly "Taekwondo"? Does Taekwondo have to be recognized by Korea to even call itself Taekwondo?

Recalling the turmoil; a rise and fall?

The best way to answer the aforementioned questions is with a simple statement of my opinion; Taekwondo much like Karate has transcended any one group and has truly become a household name. It no longer truly belongs to nor is under complete control of one group or person. While perhaps at one time in 1955, there was an effort to make Taekwondo into one unified and specific style, Taekwondo has instead grown to meet the needs of its various practitioners rather than the needs of its leaders. Perhaps what the original Korean teachers should have realized is that when you set out to spread the popularity of an entity – at some point that entity grows beyond one person's/group's direct control.

No doubt that men like Choi, Kim, and various others wanted to make Taekwondo a household name. They wanted Taekwondo to be a name that would be well-known in almost every nation's population even by those who do not practice the martial arts. And Taekwondo has succeeded in doing that. In almost every small town in the United States, one can find a Taekwondo dojang where a Korean-based martial art is practice with some of the same traditions and techniques. This is something that the early leaders of Taekwondo can be proud of.

But perhaps many of these leaders failed to realize an important lesson that history teaches us; whenever/wherever there is a rise to prominence – the entity often fails to be in the control of one person. No one man/woman can control a powerful or widespread entity on his/her own. Alexander the Great and Genghis Kahn could conquer most of the known world, but they could not control their own empire. The ancient Romans held their empire through administration and diversity, but it was ripe with one emperor after another who would be plagued by their own failures which would slowly cause Rome's fall. Even every *sa-bom* (instructor) at any dojang in the Unites States understands that if they are the sole owner and lead instructor at the school, it is easy to maintain complete control over almost every element of what is taught and how the dojang is run. But if that same instructor owns a few schools, they are forced to delegate responsibility to other instructors and their control is lessened. And if that same instructor becomes the owner of a chain of school, they almost ceased being an instructor and become more of an administrator or CEO of a corporation. It is simply a universal and natural law enforced by pure logistics.

Another universal and natural law is that any entity/system that we as human beings create and help grow all of our own faults and weaknesses often go into our creations as well as our strengths. We are imperfect beings who can only create imperfect systems, imperfect institutions, and imperfect entities. There can never be a perfect entity or system created on earth because they were created by, implemented by, and put into practice by imperfect people.

While I'm usually not one who finds wisdom from mere Hollywood movies, perhaps it can best be said with a quote from the 1959 production of *Ben-Hur* (MGM Production; Director: William Wyler). Australian character actor Frank Thring played the role of Pontius Pilate, the historic Roman governor of Judea who would eventually give the order to crucify Jesus Christ of Nazareth. In the film, Pontius Pilate is speaking with lead character Judah Ben-Hur played by Charlton Heston; and shares his harsh but pragmatic discernment. Pilate (speaking about Rome and the human cost to maintain the Roman Empire) states; *"Where there is greatness, great government or power, even great feeling or compassion, error also is great. We progress and mature by fault."*

There can be little doubt of the true greatness of the art of Taekwondo. And unfortunately it is not unique that a great art of Taekwondo is also haunted with scandal and bedlam in its relatively short history. Looking back on the art's history within just the past 60 years, it is not difficult to see all of its "greatness" and all of its "error". The art was almost literally forged out of the fire in the most difficult of times. As a newly liberated Korea was still reeling from years of oppression struggled to become a nation and culture once again, Taekwondo would be born out of that struggle. Its strength would come from determined leaders who worked tirelessly in their endeavors. Its weakness would come from the greed and corruption that often follows a rise to power.

Men like Syngman Rhee, Park Chung-Hee, Choi Hong-Hi, and Kim Un-Yong (not to mention all of their close associates) have solidified their place in South Korea's history and in the history of Taekwondo and at least perhaps many of their actions can be deemed necessary at the time. They also have solidified their place as members of the human race complete with all the sins that come with strength. Rhee was corrupt. Park was nefarious. Choi was tyrannical. And Kim was unscrupulous. Certainly those descriptions are bold and some would consider them scandalous, and there are many in Taekwondo who would disagree.

But I make those statements about those four men and about Taekwondo itself for a reason. We must remember that they are/were human beings. None of us can honestly face God or the mirror and state with absolute honesty that we have not failed, sinned, or weakened at times. And each of those men paid for their weaknesses. Rhee was disgraced and exiled. Park was killed by a trusted associate. Choi would be exiled and his family was in turmoil. And Kim served prison time and lost his position of power. They were all held accountable for their actions. And perhaps now we can look upon their deeds from a different perspective. And maybe we can look at Taekwondo itself from a different perspective as well.

The "outsider's" perspective/my own journey in Taekwondo

As mentioned in the beginning of this writing, Taekwondo is not my first art. And I can vividly remember hearing about the various scandals in the history of Taekwondo and taking a haughty attitude about the seemingly superiority of "my other martial art". Somehow I convinced myself that there was something naturally unethical about the practices of Taekwondo instructors and leadership that led to all these misgivings. Taekwondo schools were often called by other practitioners as "McDojos" or "McDojangs", a negative reference to McDonalds fast-food chain restaurants because they shared the same elements – "fast food" style martial arts with instant results but a poor product. But obviously I had not truly grown as a martial artist. I was quick to point out controversy in Taekwondo, but was blind to the sins of the leaders of my own martial art, not to mention my own. I somehow sought validity in the downfalls of other which was so misplaced. Now that I am hopefully wiser and truly a martial artist, I have come to a different conclusion.

The controversial history of Taekwondo is not unique in its imperfection. Every practitioner of Taekwondo is a human being such as all the practitioners of karate, boxing, wrestling, judo, etc. As such they are vulnerable to all the human imperfections and frailties. The organizations that oversee Taekwondo are made up of human beings who are also vulnerable to all human error. All martial arts attempt to forge a better human being, but those same human beings are at their core imperfect. Thus any scandals and controversies that may plague Taekwondo, none of the blame can be placed on Taekwondo itself. It belongs squarely on the shoulders of whoever at a specific time and place made the choice to do an unethical act. Remembering the quote from *Ben-Hu*; "we progress and mature by fault". Sometimes the best advice comes from those who've made mistakes. Some of life's best life lessons come after we've learned from the mistakes we make.

The top photos are examples of extreme elements of the martial arts including Shaolin Buddhists meditation (A) and MMA style training done by the US Army (B). While some may wish to partake in these extreme elements of the martial arts – most of us are more comfortable in the average Taekwondo dojang (C) where we can partake in the intense training with moral discipline in a family-friendly environment. This may be a vital key to the success of Taekwondo. (All photos public domain)

Maybe in that sense the art of Taekwondo is the perfect martial art for a human being. Why? Because of the fact that the art itself was codified by those who achieved both greatness and great error. *The art of Taekwondo in my opinion has become the living embodiment of all that is great and all that is not so great in human beings – thus it has become the perfect martial art for almost any card-carrying member of the human race.* From its own history we can learn so much about our potential and our potential for flaw. Hopefully in the practice of Taekwondo we can learn how to develop our strengths, and little our weaknesses. Hopefully we can learn from both the success and the scandals of the art itself.

My own journey in Taekwondo began in 2013. I had already been involved in the martial arts for a quarter of a century as a student, instructor, competitor, and researcher. My training extended to both the esoteric elements found in the traditional martial arts as well as the intense training found in the new eclectic martial arts. At the time, I honestly felt that I had reached a summit in my training and my involvement in the martial arts. If I was to dare consider myself a martial artist I would have to commit myself to two areas; a consistent search for knowledge and an ability to give back to others. At my last couple of training endeavors, while still valid I was not presented the opportunity to neither learn more nor give back to others. So I made the decision to start over. Start over as a new student; a novice. To put on a new white uniform and belt and humble myself to enter another school. But what style would I choose?

Honestly at the time I could not give a specific reason why I ended up as a Taekwondo student. On that fateful day of January 2, 2013 I began training at a school where I felt more comfortable at the given school, presented by a staff of people whom I felt to be good souls. But on that same day I would also have to consider myself a Taekwondo practitioner. And it honestly only been the last year why I think that it was the right decision to make.

Despite my long experience in the martial arts, I ultimately consider myself an average "ordinary" man. Others have given me unwarranted praise for what they consider my wisdom and insight as well as a natural ability, but I don't always see their point of view. I live what many would call a working-class lifestyle with no claims to fame and no fortunes to speak of. I've often said that I live my life by "a bunch of "F's" – <u>Faith</u> in God, <u>Fidelity</u> to my marriage, <u>Freedom</u> as an American, <u>Family</u> whom I'm loyal to, <u>Friends</u> who have my back, and the skill with the <u>Fist</u> along with the responsibility of knowing how and when to use it.

My place in the martial arts is relatively nominal. Despite many years of serious dedication to the martial arts, I am ultimately a simple man using the martial arts to better myself. Given that fact, like many of the average Americans who are involved in the martial arts I am someone who seeks out a balanced training in the martial arts to fit cohesively with my life and lifestyle. I've been a practitioner of Tai Chi Chuan and strict classical art like Okinawan Karate and found that some (not all) of the philosophy behind them was in contrasts with my Christian Faith. In addition, the arts lack any of the intense fitness training or the real life self-defense techniques that I was searching for. And yet I've also been a practitioner of free-style combative sports such as boxing and Muay Thai in addition to pure combatives skills such as Defensive Tactics. And while those arts may have provided the extreme fighting skills and intense fitness training, they lacked many of the moral discipline and philosophy that I was seeking.

In the world of martial arts there exists extreme elements such as esoteric traditional arts (left) to the modern extreme combat arts such as MMA (right). The average American generally is not made for either extreme. However most can find benefit in a more balanced art such as Taekwondo (center) which can offer the insight and discipline of the esoteric and the modern athleticism and technique of the combative arts. Taekwondo offers true balance to its practitioners. Left and right photo are public domain, center image by author.

I *believe* I can say with some certainty why the art of Taekwondo was the perfect choice for me for now as well as why it is the perfect choice for many an average American. Most of us seek both a balance of moral discipline as well as intense training. But it would generally be unwise for most of us to seek both by partaking in the extreme elements offered by strict traditional martial arts or the high intensity combat sports/combatives. Some of us may seek those extreme elements but most of us as average Americans are seeking a balance.

Also from a logistical side, most of us have full lives that we live outside the dojang. We have families and obligations and whatever martial art that we may partake in, we would surely hope that our training enhances our lives, but does not interferes with them. I've found speaking to others, that many of the more extreme elements of the martial arts (be they the esoteric or the combatives) do not necessarily lend themselves to a cohesive relationship with life outside the dojo/gym. They may require too many long hours of extreme training. They may have an almost "cult-like" atmosphere. In contrast, a great selling point for the average Taekwondo dojang is family friendly atmosphere that is conducive to the lifestyle of the average American. The dojang becomes a place where we can spend a couple hours a week enhance our lives outside the dojang. While each and every individual may have their own reason(s) for partaking in martial arts, the average person usually have some core reasons.

Generally, most of the average American will partake in the martial arts for the following reasons/personal goals;

- An understanding of basic self-defense/fighting
- An increase/maintain physical health and fitness
- A sense of mental discipline and/or focus
- A sense of personal empowerment

What most people can gain from the art of Taekwondo is a balanced approach to training in the martial arts that other arts can fail to do. This is not to say that other martial arts do not strive to meet the above mentioned goals of its practitioners; but Taekwondo does provide a more balanced approach to training to reach the goals. For example, no one can deny that an MMA gym will provide an elite level of fitness to its practitioners but the average person may not be able or willing to train at that level especially for the purpose of MMA competition. A Tai Chi/Chi Gong school may adhere to mental focus but the methodology is generally not something that the average American is willing to endure for an extended time. In short, Taekwondo provides the tools for its practitioners to meet the goals of self-defense, physical fitness, mental discipline, and personal empowerment from a balance and reasonable perspective and methodology. It could be the very key to the arts global success!

An overwhelming percentage of dojangs not only in America, but across the globe have a family friendly environment that openly caters to the training of children. The overall curriculum and training program of Taekwondo is an ideal place for empowering people at a young age. Photo is public domain.

After being a dedicated Taekwondo practitioner for almost two years as well as researching the art itself; I do believe that the greatest gift that Taekwondo offers to its students is a balance of what most of us are searching for. We (as students) are seeking many things. We are seeking fighting ability without necessarily being professional fighters. We are seeking a school of ethics but not another church. We are seeking self-discipline, not outside discipline. We are seeking sound minds and bodies, not hardened minds and bodies. And we are seeking a place to give back to not just take from. For many of us there is no better place for us than a Taekwondo dojang. There is no better place for me.

The first couple of weeks training in Taekwondo as a new and "novice" student, I have to say that I was human and I had my doubts about my decision. However it did not take long to realize that it was exactly what I was looking for. Taekwondo has become the home that I was actively seeking. The Taekwondo dojang is place to continue learning; partaking in the intense physical training while still training my mind in moral and ethical discipline. And it has become a place where I can also give back to the other student by sharing with them the knowledge that I have gathered over the years. In fact my previous experience was not a hindrance, it was a blessing. The overall structure and curriculum of Taekwondo was open to incorporating my other skills. It was those skills that I was able to share with the other students and hopefully aid them in their training and personal goals. I have once again become both a student and an instructor with the art of Taekwondo being the new home.

Photo by author

Perspective

Taekwondo undoubtedly possesses a most unique history. Despite its meager 60-year history, Taekwondo's story is rich with all of human kind's triumphs and failures, strengths and weaknesses. It was an art forge in the fire of a very tumultuous time in history, but it was that fire that perhaps gave Taekwondo its true strength. The result was a martial art that has become one of the most popular in the world. We can learn from both the success and failures of many of Taekwondo's pioneers because both success and failure is a part of the human experience. Taekwondo is an art that offers its practitioners a balanced training of both fighting and discipline. And rather than link the art to the ancient Korean warriors, we should focus on Taekwondo's history within the past 60 years because it was that modern history that truly made it a martial art for the modern human being.

From an outsider's perspective, I believe the history of Taekwondo is unique as the art itself. It's a history that I am taking part in, but I am still an outsider partially by choice, but also by circumstance.

Perhaps some of it is my fault. Despite diving head first into my journey of Taekwondo, ultimately I have a hard time getting the fisticuffs brawler mentality out of my head. With that mentality comes an unwavering desire to look at all things from a harsh realistic point of view instead of "fantasyland" perspective. It is too much a part of me. But any life experience can be a learning experience as well. And I've experience Taekwondo firsthand. I may not be learning anything new in terms of technique or discipline, but in examining the history of Taekwondo, I am gaining a better perspective about human nature. The controversial history of Taekwondo is something that anyone can learn from even if it's nothing more than what to avoid and what not to do!

Afterthoughts

So fast forward to present day; it has been a couple of years since my journey in Taekwondo ended at the tail end of 2016. A mere three years total, my participation in Taekwondo was relatively short but quite full. I had started as a novice, earned my first degree black belt, became an instructor, took the bronze medal at a championship tournament, earned my second degree black belt, and became a co-owner at the school I trained at.

I will be the first to admit that the journey ended due to the fact that *I* left. The dynamic changed with the school joining the aforementioned world organization which offered no support at all. Later after a severed relationship, there was a push from the other partners to rejoin the organization again. The school was run as a three-partner LLC with me being one of the partners. I have no doubt that all of us (the three partners) will have a different opinion as to why the school eventually failed but what I can say is that I warned the others that changes would need to be made if the school was to survive. My warning was never heeded and it took a matter of months before my premonition came true. But honestly I had voluntarily left just prior to the closing of the school.

The reader now may understandably come to the conclusion that somehow I am basically just sore at the art and leadership of Taekwondo and am I now using my old thesis as platform to discredit the art. Nothing could be further from the truth. I still stand by the words I mentioned in my 2014 essay, particularly the later portion discussing the balance that Taekwondo offers the average American. I still have respect for the art itself and I believe I know why the art was flourishing. But I also believe I know why it is massively faltering in recent times.

I know that last sentence sounds a bit harsh, but it is unfortunately true. Taekwondo as an art has faltered. And it has faltered quite hard. It has in fact failed many of the students of the art itself. The failure has manifested itself in the falling number of both students worldwide and falling number of schools. There will be a great deal of debate if Taekwondo is actually losing popularity and if schools have been in fact closing at an alarming rate. There are no verified systems to show exact student numbers of every martial arts school based on style. Even the popular "Google trends" which matches how often people will search for a specific subject is flawed in determining if Taekwondo is falling in popularity.

There is however a general consensus that traditional martial arts or more specifically traditional Asian-based martial arts, are greatly losing ground to other entities such as mixed martial arts (MMA), reality-based self-defense, or new athletic systems such as CrossFit. Being that Taekwondo stood as the world's most popular of the traditional Asian-based martial arts, it is only fair to examine it as a model of why the traditional martial arts are losing ground. It is my opinion based on someone who has lived as a life-long martial artists that are three major reasons as to why the traditional Asian-based martial arts have fallen, and more specifically why the art of Taekwondo has fallen;

- The Asian martial arts/Taekwondo have lost their "mystique"
- The rise of other systems/athletic activities
- The dominate culture of tyrannical world organizations in Taekwondo

While the first two reason may be relevant to other traditional Asian martial arts as well, the last one is completely unique to Taekwondo.

Taekwondo has lost its "mystique"

Before continuing, we should define "mystique" as related to the martial arts. Probably the best way is to use the example of the legendary martial art icon Bruce Lee. When you hear the name "Bruce Lee", what comes to mind? It is likely that of an almost superhuman being with the physical speed and power beyond comprehension. He was truly the "deadliest man the world has ever know". If you recall all the iconic images that he helped create through his movies, they could be considered as part of the "mystique" of Bruce Lee. The "reality" of Bruce Lee was far different. He was born to overall poor physical health, suffered debilitating injuries in his young life, didn't always practice what he preached, did not have many years of formal martial arts training, was just an actor by trade late in his life, and died at a very young age. And even when one looks at his teachings early in his life; Bruce Lee was not attempting to demonstrate some sort of "ancient Chinese magical secret" to his students. Instead he primarily focused on pioneering what he considered real fighting and self-knowledge. That is the reality of Bruce Lee, a far cry from the mystique of Bruce Lee. I'm not criticizing Bruce Lee. The fact that he was *not* superhuman makes his real life accomplishments all the more impressive.

All Asian-based martial arts have lost their mystique, including Taekwondo. Gone are the days when the general public in America believed that the traditional Asian-based martial arts were the pinnacle fighting systems where the practitioners could almost perform magic. But in truth, they never should have had any mystique at all. From the first day that karate, judo, or Taekwondo was taught in the United States, it should have been seen from a far more realistic perspective. Unfortunately the Asian-based martial arts have culturally always thrived on a mythology. And years ago that same mythology was repeated to potential American students for the purpose of advertising.

To illustrate this to the reader, I'm going to list a number of facts that counter many of the martial arts myths because the historic record and/or existing evidence does not support these myths or completely contradicts them;

- There is no evidence of the existence of "chi" (Chinese) or "Ki" (Japanese)

- There is no evidence that the legendary Buddhist Bodhidharma had anything to do with the creation of the martial arts.
- The legend of the black belt and belt system is not from the myth of never washing ones' belt so it starts changing colors. The evidence suggests that Judo Founder Jigoro Kano first introduced it inspired from western athletic education.
- The breaking of boards, bricks, and ice have nothing to do with metaphysics – but actually with both basic physics and occasional trickery
- " some sort of "secret magic" to their students and certainly did not intend to initiate them into their "secret warrior culture". I believe in their own way they were simply trying to offer their students a number of skills that they deemed pragmatic; a method of intense physical, mental, and emotional training to better themselves. Their art had benefited them personally and they wanted to share the benefits with others, plain and simple.

If I had to pick two critical years where the traditional Asian-based martial arts began to lose their mystique it would 1984 and 1993. 1984 would be the year that the traditional Asian-based martial arts would find a new economic market which forced them to be more pragmatic. And 1993 would be the year that the traditional martial arts would be forced to live up to their hype and ultimately fail.

1984 was the year that Columbia Pictures released the film *The Karate Kid* (Delphi II Productions/Jerry Weintraub Productions; Directed by John G. Avildsen). The movie not only help popularize the traditional Asian-based martial arts, but it also exposed another element about the martial arts itself. For the first time to the general American public the martial arts would be seen as more than just a fighting art solely for adults. Parents began to see the martial arts as the perfect system of physical training along with mental discipline for their kids. The martial arts industry reacted almost immediately and the "cash cow" for the traditional Asian-based martial arts became kids programs. In and of itself there was certainly nothing wrong with that. However as the traditional Asian-based martial arts began to be run more like a business, it forced them to become pragmatic.

Taekwondo took ahold of the opportunity to offer kids programs as the predominant student body in Taekwondo schools became children and teens. That eliminated some of the mystique as Taekwondo instructors could not sell paying parents that they were turning their kids into killing machines. Most Taekwondo instructors sell their concepts of mental discipline or sold the concept of "empowerment" without in my opinion actually focusing on it or actually defining it. But possibly the biggest mistake that just about all Taekwondo schools did was to make the coveted black belt a lot easier to obtain.

Taekwondo is notorious for giving black belts to young kids after a mere two years of training while selling it as a mark of mastery. What many Taekwondo practitioners probably don't realize is how much of the mystique of Taekwondo was lost with the practice of kids earning a black belt after a short couple of years. Here's cold hard question: how in the world can an 8-year-old kid be a black belt *if* a black belt in Taekwondo is supposed to be the mark of mature person who is proficient in both discipline and fighting? If an art has an established practice of giving their mark of mastery to children, then how much credibility in the area of fighting and self-defense can a Taekwondo black belt have? The best evidence for this argument is the often touted fact that out of all the students who earned their 1st degree black belt in Taekwondo, only a small fraction will actually go on to earn their 2nd degree black belt. Why? In my opinion because they may feel that the art truly has nothing more to teach outside of more material to learn. They already earned the "prestige" they were looking for in the black belt, so why continue in something that is not truly offering them anything?

1993 would be the year that the Ultimate Fighting Championship (UFC) would host its first tournament in Denver, Colorado. Created by Rorion Gracie and Art Davis, it was designed to showcase which martial art was the "ultimate" martial art. The UFC was certainly not the legitimate sports entity that has become today. But even at the time what the UFC demonstrated with both the inaugural tournament and the subsequent tournaments is that the mystique of the traditional Asian-based martial arts was a lie. Overwhelmingly the traditional Asian-based martial artists in the early UFC tournaments were beaten so badly by those who generally practiced a more freestyle combative sport or a more modern eclectic martial art. When a so-called traditional martial artists had any success at all it was not from traditional techniques but appeared to be more from any level of street fighting experience that they might have had.

As the UFC helped create the sport of mixed martial arts (MMA), the traditional Asian-based martial arts had to separate themselves completely from anything resembling real fighting. Most Taekwondo schools like to believe that they are different from the other traditional Asian-based martial arts based on the fact that their art partakes in modern athletic tournaments such as the Olympics. But the truth is most Taekwondo schools are in fact traditional. And in being traditional, Taekwondo itself has lost its mystique.

Taekwondo is facing fierce competition from other athletic activities

With MMA becoming a legitimate and recognized sport, MMA-type gyms have been on the rise. In comparison to a Taekwondo dojang, MMA gyms arguably offer students higher intensity physical training and still offers a degree of discipline. Some might scoff at the idea of an MMA gym offering any sort of moral, emotional, or mental discipline that is equal to that of Taekwondo. However the discipline that any combative sport offers its practitioners is almost automatic based on logistics. In order to have success in the combative sports you must work hard, heed to your coach/instructor, and have respect for your training partners. It also greatly depends on the individual instructor and has nothing to do with the art itself.

The more intense training in MMA can also be seen as being closer to real life as opposed to Taekwondo. Life can be hard. It requires a lot of work that will likely cost you blood, sweat, and tears. Unlike the system of Taekwondo, in MMA you don't earn accolades just because you've been participating for a while memorizing prearranged movements. Most goals achieved in real life don't come with the pomp and circumstance like that of a black belt test. Combative sports such as boxing, wrestling, Muay Thai, MMA, and to a large part Brazilian Jiu Jitsu generally have a more realistic feel not only in their training but in the ambiance in the gyms themselves. This is due in large part because there are no real titles of "master" or "grandmaster". Both instructors and students earn their own accolades by achieving their personal goals. They don't sit on any manufactured laurels but rather stand on their own personal accomplishments. Even if the gym has some sort of grading system such as colored belts, the rank is secondary to the actual training and competing.

In recent years both adults and kids have also found various other athletic activities that can offer them all the same benefits that they might have sought in traditional Asian-based martial arts training. For adults things such as CrossFit, yoga, and cycling offer the participants the level of physical fitness that traditional Asian-based martial arts use to offer as well as a degree of mental and emotional discipline that is required for participation and success. For kids it can be everything from varsity sports, extreme sports, and other activities that offer them the same physical, mental, and emotional discipline that they might have gotten at a traditional Asian-based martial arts school like Taekwondo.

But what specifically is it about the modern western martial arts as well other athletic activities that are drawing people away from the traditional Asian-based martial arts? Is there some sort of advantages they have over something like Taekwondo? In my opinion yes. In an activity such as Taekwondo as a whole, there is an overwhelming goal of the participant to essentially only become better Taekwondo practitioners – not necessarily better martial artists or people. Most dojangs focus so much only on the standard Taekwondo curriculum that the innate goal for every student and instructor becomes to meet the strict standards of the art. Thus the practitioner lives to serve and better *the art*. But it should be the other way around, the art should serve and better *the practitioner.*

Another reason why other physical activities are replacing Taekwondo is the lack of false grandeur. An unfortunate truth about Taekwondo is that it is full of ostentation and fake pageantry, probably more than any other Asian-based martial arts. The strict uniform guidelines, the pretentious titles of the leaders, and the flamboyancy at the larger testing and tournaments are just a few examples. Overwhelmingly most of the Taekwondo organization insist on presenting themselves as some sort of regal art from. The overall result is a feeling of pompousness that is completely unwarranted and unnecessary. Most Americans don't feel the need to have a false sense of royalty because there is no such thing as royalty to us, nor should there be.

The truth is that some black belts are worth more than others based on the work that the instructor and student put into training, not based on the false prestige of the organization that certifies them. It is my opinion that some black belts are marks of achievement while others are just useless! (Photo by author)

The first black belt I earned was in the art Kenpo. My Kenpo instructor always insisted that he simply used the Kenpo system to teach his students but his curriculum was literally anything and everything that he deemed to be useful without the "fancy mess". He had black belts in a number of different martial arts and given the rank that he earned, tradition would have allowed him to give himself some sort of exalted title. But when he taught he insisted you just call him by his first name. He focused on developing the student. His black belt test was a long physical and mental endeavor where I had to not only demonstrate that I knew material, but could also adapt it for myself. The "test" was over a couple of days but I didn't even know it was a test. A few days later, he came to my home to tell me that he had a gift for me. There was no ceremony and no pageant and I was actually wearing sweats at the time. He often joked that I was not earning my black belt in Kenpo or Kung Fu – but in "Matt Fu".

By contrast my second degree black belt in Taekwondo was completely different. There was no sacred teacher-student relationship. There was no real sense of personal goals or accomplishment. It was just all ceremony. A very bloated ceremony with all the pompous snobbery and fake pageantry. There was panels and panels of "officials" along with banner flags and "international representatives" from Korea. It was topped off with a "knighting" ceremony of every student followed by a tea ceremony. At the end they told you that you were earning their prestige. But that so-called prestige of a black belt and certificate came with an expensive price tag that was just not worth it.

This is an element of Taekwondo that is losing students in the United States. Americans are practical people who care about what they spend their hard earned money on. Paying hundreds of dollars to attend a pompous ceremony and given "prestige" is not economical for most Americans. They would much rather spend the same money to become a member at a local freestyle gym where there is no ceremony or false prestige but just honest hard work to achieve the goals that they set as individuals, not the goals set by an art or organization.

Big organizations are collapsing Taekwondo from inside

This is by far my biggest contention with Taekwondo and what I feel is the number one reason that the art is both suffering in success and failing the students. No other traditional Asian-based martial art or any art is so tyrannically controlled by world organizations with ties to government entities and corrupt scandals than Taekwondo. That is just a cold hard fact. And with that fact comes the harsh reality that Taekwondo is collapsing from inside.

As previously mentioned, Taekwondo is pretty much controlled by the two big organizations; the International Taekwondo Federation (ITF) and the World Taekwondo Federation (WTF). At the time that I wrote the original thesis the ITF was in disarray with three separate groups all claiming control of the Choi's original organization and the WTF was still recovering from their scandals. In-between the time of the original thesis and this current writing, a number of changes took place but not necessarily for the betterment of Taekwondo.

The ITF and WTF went on a public relations campaign that they essentially agreed to an almost "peace treaty" by recognizing one another and allowing all members of both groups to attend any tournaments put on by the ITF or WTF. I believe this is a hollow gesture at best as both organizations are more interested in holding onto their fledgling power. There have also been a number of lawsuits made against the Kukkiwon by US-based Taekwondo groups. I've even read some unverified reports that Taekwondo is losing its popularity in both North and South Korea in recent years. With the Panmunjom Declaration officially ending the Korean War this year, both nations and their people have more important issues to deal with than controlling the destiny of their "national art" of Taekwondo.

Whatever the reports it must be said that Taekwondo has no danger of completely collapsing anytime soon. Nor are the two large organizations in any danger of going bankrupt in the near future. But I do believe that Taekwondo will continue to lose not only the number of students, but its prestige so long as the large organizations continue to rule the art with an iron fist and continue their almost Mafioso-style extortion of small local Taekwondo schools.

Allow me to share one of my personal experiences. It was towards the end of my Taekwondo journey. I had already spent a huge amount of money for the disappointing pomp and circumstance in receiving my 2nd degree black belt from the unnamed world organization in

Taekwondo. During that testing, the organization was obviously doing everything they could to kowtow to their Korean representatives from both the Kukkiwon and the WTF. They placed new demands on all the students in an effort to appease the representatives just short of groveling to them – or perhaps they did grovel!

In any event, by this point the school had left the organization but my business partners were considering rejoining them. I attempted to stay open minded and agreed to a conference with the CEO of the Taekwondo organization. The CEO had made it openly clear that the goal of his organization was to garner immense favor with both the Kukkiwon and the WTF in Korea at almost any cost. During the conference I asked some blunt questions and got very political and diplomatic answers. One question I specifically asked was, "knowing all the political and criminal scandals attached to both the Kukkiwon and the WTF why would anyone want to be a part of either organization especially when they seemingly don't really offer anything to the local Taekwondo schools in the US?" The CEO answered like a true politician using what I would call lawyer tricks; answering questions with baiting questions.

He listed a series of those questions to my one question; why be a part of a corrupt entity? "Well, you wouldn't want an unlicensed doctor performing surgery on you would you? You know some of the dark history of the US, do you still love your country? You're not saying you're perfect are you?" Of course those are not answers to my question, they're just baiting arguments. The more emotional among us may rally around arguments in a debate because it feeds their feelings. But the more rational among us know that arguments have nothing to do with answers and it's a vain attempt to simply redirect with the false sense of a moral high ground.

I certainly could have shot down any of his arguments with truth; "there's a vast different between Taekwondo training and brain surgery, of course I love my country which is why I work to improve it, no I'm not perfect but I'm not foolish to join a corrupt organization". Instead of just being baited in I instead focused on cold truth telling him, "None of those arguments have anything to do with my question that you have still not answered"!

In the same meeting one of my partners asked the question about our recent black belt test inquiring that our certificates from their organizations did not include certification from the Kukkiwon; something that they were actively advertising at the time. The CEO made a lane excuse about it but then essentially stated that he could make "special arrangements" to have us recognized by the Kukkiwon *if* we rejoined their organization, and paid a little money for the trouble. Suddenly now their illusion of selling prestige became clear to me. We essentially didn't grovel enough to their organization or pay enough thus we weren't worthy for the prestige of the Kukkiwon. But if we somehow "saw the error of our ways" and rejoined them, the prestige could be given to us with a little political wrangling and some more money… as a bribe!

The Taekwondo dojang was part of a three-person LLC, and as only one of three partners my vote was obviously beaten in the decision to rejoin the organization. However the organization did nothing to stave off the eventual closure of the school and in my opinion, it helped cause it.

Big organizations might be necessary to coordinate and promote sports tournaments, but they should in no way extort, dictate, or control a local school for the illusion of prestige. There are number of organization that are responsible for hosting amateur and professional sporting tournaments, but none of them control how every individual school is to be run nor do they attempt to siphon additional money out of the schools outside of services rendered. A successful instructor does not need titles or prestige. A successful school does not need a connection to some organization. Their success comes from the success of the students they teach either, a well-deserved reputation, and/or a constant work ethic/business mind which cumulates into economic success. There is something fundamentally good about real capitalism because it demonstrates individual freedom and choices. But there is something fundamentally wrong with a tyrannical system using market economics couple with cronyism. There is something fundamentally wrong with that model; the model of organizations like the ITF, the WTF, and the Kukkiwon.

Conclusion

So it has been a couple of years since I left the Taekwondo dojang that I once considered my training grounds. I've returned to my previous boxing gym and my freestyle combative sports ways. In addition I take every opportunity to learn, research and attend training seminars not just in the field of martial arts but also in areas such defensive tactics, personal safety, use of force in the law, and defensive pistol and shotgun. By in large all my training today has far more realistic and pragmatic value than my previous Taekwondo training. And I don't have to refer to anyone as "master" or "grandmaster" instead just using terms such as coach, trainer, instructor, or friend by first name.

But I'd be lying if I said that I didn't miss Taekwondo. Mostly in that it did offer me a perfect arena to share and teach young people. Many of my peers felt that in the classes that I taught, I wasn't really teaching them Taekwondo and perhaps that is true. But I made sure that everything I did teach young people was both useful and fun. And my number one goal was to help them achieve their personal goals whatever they happened to be. As I told one promising student, "my goal is not to make you as good as me. It's to make you better. And the ultimate reward for me as an instructor would be to look you in the eye and say that I honestly have no more to teach you. Go out and seek more knowledge… from another instructor!"

That perhaps is the greatest tragedy of Taekwondo in my opinion. As I mentioned previously in my thesis portion, Taekwondo does stand poised to be the perfect platform for young people to partake in a combative sport and martial art. I don't even fault the sports elements of Taekwondo the way others may critique it for not being "more realistic" as opposed to sports like MMA. Sport Taekwondo is a combative sport like any other. It can serve as a relatively safe platform for kids and adults to partake in offering them a competitive endeavor. The problem is in order to anyone to partake in the sport they must be a Taekwondo student at a school certified by the WTF or ITF or by one of the umbrella organizations and must be ranked by the same organization which pays all the organization fees. The process can be a little stifling.

In a perfect world it would be so much more beneficial for each and every Taekwondo school to be free to teach their students as each individual instructor saw fit as well as possibly incorporating other arts and other training methods. That participation in Taekwondo tournaments could be open to any martial arts school willing to abide to tournament rules, with or without Kukkiwon, WTF, or ITF membership. It would also be beneficial to allow Taekwondo students to participate in other martial arts tournaments according to other rules. It would enable the art of Taekwondo to flourish and grow to meet the needs of the ever changing students instead of forcing students to conform to Taekwondo standards.

Yes perhaps I'm contradicting myself because as a realists I know that there is no such thing as a perfect world. And the turmoil in the art of Taekwondo is nothing new or unique. But perhaps I saw so much potential and scandal in the same entity which made me realize that the real history of Taekwondo as told from the perspective of an outsider had so many lessons in it. They are lessons of greatness and great error. They are lessons that other martial arts styles and entities can learn from; what to do and what not to do. The history of Taekwondo is in fact a model of all human success and human failures.

The history of Taekwondo is a history that I played such a miniscule part of that might be worth a footnote if I'm lucky. But I was a part of Taekwondo for a time. But now once again, I'm an outsider. I'm an outsider who can give his perspective on the history of Taekwondo!

Annotated Bibliography

Web Resources;

- www.ataonline.com/history
- www.itftkd.org/about
- www.koreataekwondo.org/encyclopedia
- www.worldtaekwondofederation.net/
- www.wikipedia.org

Written Resources;

Choi, General Hong Hi *The Encyclopedia of Taekwon-do Volumes 1-15* Ontario, Canada International Taekwon-do Federation 1983

Cook, Doug *Traditional Taekwondo* Boston, Massachusetts YMAA Publication Center 2006

Crudelli, Cris *The Way of the Warrior* London, UK Dorling Kindersley 2008

Dohrenwend, Robert Ph.D. *Taekwondo: A Historic Appraisal* Classical Fighting Arts/Dragon Times Magazine 2003

Gillis, Alex *A Killing Art; the Untold History of Taekwondo* Toronto, Ontario Canada ECW Press 2008

Kano, Jigoro *Mind over Muscle* Tokyo, Japan Kodansha International 2005

Kim, Sang H. Ph.D. *The Comprehensive Illustrated Manual of Martial Arts of Ancient Korea* Wethersfield, CT Turtle Press 2000

Lee, Ki-baik *A New History of Korea* Seoul, Korea Ilchokak Publishers 1984

Lee, Myong Kyong *Taekwondo Philosophy and Culture* Elizabeth, NJ Hollym International 2001

Park, Yeon Hwan Gerrard, Jon *Black Belt Taekwondo* New York, NY Checkmark Books 2000

Yates, Keith D. *The Complete Guide to American Karate and Taekwondo* Berkley, CS Blue Snake Books 2008

Printed in Great Britain
by Amazon